I Knew
I Was Right

JULIE BURCHILL

I Knew
I Was Right

An Autobiography

HEINEMANN : LONDON

First published in Great Britain 1998
by William Heinemann

1 3 5 7 9 10 8 6 4 2

Random House UK Limited
20 Vauxhall Bridge Road, London SW1V 2SA

Random House Australia (Pty) Limited
20 Alfred Street, Milsons Point, Sydney,
New South Wales 2061, Australia

Random House New Zealand Limited
18 Poland Road, Glenfield
Auckland 10, New Zealand

Random House South Africa (Pty) Limited
Endulini, 5a Jubilee Road, Parktown 2193, South Africa

Random House UK Limited Reg. No. 954009

A CIP catalogue record for this book
is available from the British Library

Papers used by Random House UK Limited are natural, recyclable products
from wood grown in sustainable forests. The manufacturing processes
conform to the environmental regulations of the country of origin.

ISBN 0434 000795

Typeset by SX Composing DTP, Rayleigh, Essex
Printed and bound in Great Britain by
Mackay's of Chatham plc, Chatham, Kent

For Charlotte R

With all the love and thanks in the world to Peter
York, John Linsdell, Laura Lockington and my
poor, sainted parents

Never eat anything you can't lift
Miss Piggy

Golly
at Noon

It was hot that day. High-summer hot, High Noon hot, Howdy Stranger hot. But sadly, I was no Gary Cooper.

Rather, I was a Golly. A Golly at Noon.

At the age of ten, I walked up the busy main road my parents lived on to my Brownie troupe's annual fancy-dress parade, dressed as a Robertson Golly. My Auntie Dolly Brain worked at the famous jam factory and so was allowed to borrow such outlandish garb for young relations. That Saturday I wore a red satin jacket, striped satin trousers (blue and yellow), an Afro wig which swelled my small head to twice its normal size, and jet-black face and hands, thanks to the Leichner stage make-up my father had pitilessly tracked down. 'If a job's worth doing . . .' My father was a trades union agitator in the days when we as a family generally, and he specifically, were gleefully spending 24:7 holding the country to ransom and revelling in our new-found power; when clearing out a factory in record time during a spot of secondary picketing, my father would appeal, with no apparent irony intended, to the workers' buried sense of vocation by reminding them that 'If a job's worth doing, it's worth doing well!' Nothing was guaranteed to have them downing tools faster.

Two cars crashed. A pregnant lady ran screaming, her Dr Scholl sandal coming off. Oddly, I picked it up solemnly and carried on;

a small Gollywog Prince Charming, searching for a sloppy, swollen-ankled Cinderella.

The alleged Hell's Angels (the recognised leader of the pack kept a large and beautifully maintained aviary in his parents' garden, which for some reason rendered him even more menacing) outside our local hostelry the Good Intent – what the road to hell is paved with, apparently; irony of ironies, considering the course my life was to take – had a field day. 'Go back to Africa!' 'Enoch Rules!' This was the year Blue Mink's 'Melting Pot' was a smash hit; boys at the local comprehensive would beat up Ugandan Asians on the way home from school and play that, or reggae, on pub juke-boxes in the evening. Yes, life was certainly already shaping up chock-full of ironies. Except then I didn't know the word. I just thought it was a mistake.

The abuse and naked mockery of small children followed me the whole half-mile. A catcalling caravan formed behind me, straggling and half-hearted as everything seemed to be in the Bristol of my youth; living, loving, losing, beating up anyone the wrong side of beige. They weren't *bad* people, it seemed to me then, simply because they couldn't be *bothered*.

Eventually their spawn peeled off sharply in non-specific dismay, not really knowing what they had expected a Golly at Noon to do anyway.

I walked on in stony silence, strangely unmoved. And, if I believed in epiphanies, I would have had one then; I would have realised that the astonishment, hostility and dismay of onlookers were to be my lot in life. And that, out of these, I would make something almost brilliant.

I came second and beat up Red Riding Hood, the winner.

CHAPTER ONE

It's
Alive!

It is widely if mutely acknowledged these days that babies are the bald, beautiful bailiffs of romantic love. If things are looking shaky to start with, they will step stumblingly in, hanging on to the edges of the furniture all the while and bring the toppling tower of bricks to a merciful end.

Having children accentuates more marital faults than adultery does; this may be why one in three young women no longer wants a little bundle of joy except on a purely time-sharing, best-friend's-brat, afternoon-out type of arrangement – *a baby is just for Christmas: not for life*! In fact, if a marriage can survive children, it can survive anything.

With this sad fact in mind, I regard through misty eyes the marriage of my parents, Bill and Bette Burchill of Bristol. Their marriage – always a pleasure, never a duty – has survived some forty-five summers.

And me.

When I read the Births announcements in the unpopular press, a Mother Goose walks over my grave and I give myself up momentarily to the squirmy masochistic glee – almost sexual in its wounding warmth – of imagining just how, with the benefit of hindsight, my parents might have announced *their* happy arrival. I don't really think it would have been at all heavy on the 'delighted to announce' or '*Deo gratias*'. I think perhaps that it might have featured a line drawing of a competent if humourless stork carrying a bouncing bald baby in a makeshift sling accompanied with the words *Why oh why?* or *Why us, God?* or even the timeless classic *There is no God*.

Anyway, the deed was done. I was born into the flaming crucible of July 1959, the hottest summer of our shimmering century. And my unfortunate parents were left alone by the criminally irresponsible doctors and nurses of Southmead Hospital, Bristol, to get on with the job of raising me. They were plain, good people who were used to walking in the ways of the Lord; my father was a Stalinist and my mother worshipped Bette Davis. So far as we knew, there was no Martian blood on either side of the family. It might have been easier if those devil-child films – *It's Alive, Demon Seed, Damien* – had been on popular release then. But it was the dreamy, serene Somerset city of Bristol, built on the blood of slavery, and there was no cavalry coming, no exorcism to hand and no way out. So they did the only thing they could do in the circumstances; they raised me.

And they raised me well, very well. Because you have to consider *how much worse* I could have been if they had neglected, warped or abused me. In years to come, both my husbands and my beloved Charlotte Raven would accuse me of being a psychopath or, if they were in a good mood, a sociopath. Charlotte Raven, after a particularly nasty bit of treachery on my part, said that she could not hear about the trial of the mass murderer Rose West without thinking of her own true love's *little something missing* and concluding that, but for the grace of God and the sheer goodness of my parents, it might easily have been me down in that cellar, up in that dock. I thought this was a bit on the judgemental side and told her so.

But the *little something missing* is a fact and I cannot say for the life of me where it came from, or where it went. Looking back to my babyhood, I find no clues whatsoever and can only come to the conclusion that I was indeed born bad. And that somehow, *somehow*, my talent, such as it is, has given me a life rather than the expected life sentence.

4

Just as blind people have extraordinarily good hearing, sociopaths apparently are often blessed with hyper-human qualities: charm, affection, generosity. I cannot pass a beggar without clutching his or her hand, pressing a note of large denomination in it (so large, often, that the sweet beggar in question will back away, shaking its head, thinking, quite rightly, that they've got *a right nutter here*), murmuring 'My brother/sister' and walking away weeping, the world a blur of shame before me. When in love, I become a geisha, as dirty and as pure as that implies. As a patron of those younger, poorer and less talented than myself, which includes pretty much the whole damn world if we're being honest here, I simply cannot do enough to help.

But. If ever I am in a position in which I must choose to pursue my own pleasure and thereby break one or more innocent hearts and lives of those close to me, or to forgo that pleasure and keep the hearts and lives of loved ones intact, there simply is no choice. In such a scenario, I feel – and here I must take a deep breath – that literally no one matters but me. If it ain't broke, *break it* would seem to be my design for living.

Reading this back, I suppose it's sort of shocking to confess to psychopathy so early on in the game, but whenever I read autobiographies, no matter how excellent they are, I am struck by how little of a handle most people have on themselves. Their promiscuity is justified as eternal romanticism, their incessant swilling as the tortured soul seeking sanctuary in a Scotch bottle, their avarice as a natural outcome of being forced to sleep in a shoebox with two other siblings when young. Well, I'm not saying I won't lie about anything during the course of this memoir. I'll lie a lot – about other people, that is. I'll lie about them and try to make them seem better than they were because if I showed them in all their swinishness I would look like the blind lemon of all time for giving them the time of day, let alone sleeping with them.

But I won't lie about myself. Why should I? One of the terrific things about being a sociopath – and it must be said that there are quite a few; my friend Susan Raven once scolded me, 'Just because you're a psychopath, young lady, *don't think it means you can do what you want!*', which it does, of course – is that you just don't give a damn what anyone thinks of you.

'You're not human!' Charlotte Raven once screamed at me.

'I wouldn't lower myself,' I replied.

And also, it's good to throw in a bit of adult material, and psychopathy *is* dead glam on paper, if not in real life when it is as numbing and monotonous as any other sort of mental glitch for those who have to cope with it. However interesting a biography, wading through those oceans of unknown relations who blight every icon's childhood is the literate equivalent of watching other people's home movies. And in nine times out of ten they turn out to have less bearing on the overall development of the book's subject than an infant toe-stubbing incident in a local and ill-attended lido late one summer. You bought this book to read about me, not my Auntie Dolly, wondrous though she is. So it's me you're getting. I, Sociopath.

Scattered clues to my condition seem to glint like lethal, gleaming, gum-cutting coins in the pungent, comforting Christmas pud of my infanthood as I look back in languor. Bald as a baby alien, for the first year of my life I was not permitted to be perambulated in public without benefit of a bonnet to hide my shiny shame lest strollers mocked. My sexual identity, in the bleak days before bonnets were many, was called copiously into question by passers-by who would congratulate my mother on her 'beautiful little boy'. As terrified of gender-blurring as any good soldier, she thus confined me to barracks until the correct millinery could put me back on the straight-and-narrow pramway.

Bald, bald . . . bald as the Roswell alien. Seeing the first photographs of the creature in 1995, I cried myself stupid before an astounded Raven family who put themselves through agonies of explanation as to why the Roswell pictures were false. But I was inconsolable. Other girls, from Debbie Harry down, have convinced themselves that they might be the bastard daughters of Marilyn Monroe. Well, I know it sounds strange, and probably a lie, but I felt that way seeing the photograph of the Roswell alien and its poor, gashed leg – that it might have been my mother. And

I its poor alien child, doomed to wander a world not mine to understand. No wonder I'm a bit of a psycho. Look at poor Jerome Newton in *The Man Who Fell To Earth*. So my husbands and my lady love think I'm a freak, do they, then? Hmmm. They're lucky I didn't take my nipples off on our wedding night, is all.

It was around this time, tellingly, that my father began to take a keen interest in science fiction. Before my birth he had only had time for Westerns – what we called 'cowboy films'. You might think this a strange taste for a Stalinist, and a wildly anti-American Stalinist at that. But Stalin was actually very fond of Westerns himself and characteristically put them to use as instruments of torment as well as sources of entertainment. Whenever he wanted to off a henchman, just to break the monotony he'd have them round to his place for an all-night session of Western movies. First one to yawn bought the building. My dad's absolute heroes were Stalin and John Wayne; the only time I saw him in any way distressed by a film – not counting *Little Women*; immense blubbering every time Margaret O'Brien joined the majority – was when he saw *Big Jim McLain*, in which John Wayne hunts out American Communists. My dad didn't know where to put himself; he was like a woman running two boyfriends and they both turn up on the doorstep at once.

My father was christened Thomas William but everyone always called him Bill. Bill seems to suit him to the nth degree; he *is* 'My Bill', the 'ordinary guy' of the Berlin song whom the heroine damns with faint praise all the way through, before soaringly confessing at the end, 'I *love* him / Because he's *wonderful* / Because he's *just my Bill*.' Rodgers and Hammerstein had his number too, in *Carousel*, when 'My Boy Bill' was imagined as being 'strong and as tall as a tree' and impossible to push around. In all my life I have never met another man who actually was a gentle giant, a man of such great physical ability and confidence that issues of masculinity were completely foreign to him. He managed my mother – a fascinating woman but volatile to say the least, forever jumping over backyard fences in order to throttle her ex-best friends – without once raising his voice, let alone his hand.

In later life I was to meet men who would raise both at the slightest show of spirit on my part and it made me think that it really wasn't such a good idea to encourage men to express their feelings; it just means that they get to yell at you and hit you even more. I wish men were like they used to be. Until they are, I'll continue to go out only with women and boys.

But anyway, here is Just My Bill fairly soaking up the old sci-fi, after showing no interest whatsoever. He would pore for hours over crude pictorial representations of alleged aliens, no doubt casting many an askance glance at my smooth young head. And there were other signs that I was not quite as I should be; my silent, violent bouts of blind destruction, perhaps. I was by all accounts a good baby, who slept soundly all night and played happily all day, rejecting more obvious toys in favour of picture books – apparently, from the first, I loved my books beyond all understanding. Until one day when my mother entered my room to find me standing bald and livid in my pink matinée coat and matching bootees, chubby hands gripping the rail of my cot, face grim and staring. And all around me, in a tickertape blizzard of home-made confetti, swirled my beloved books.

My mother, Bette, née Thomas, had had a rotten time until she met my dad. Her gentle mother died when she was very young, but her drunken father stuck around, making her life a misery, making her life *not her own*, as adults do when they deprive children of their childhoods. When he stumbled off this mortal coil, she was sent to live with an evil aunt-and-uncle combo straight from Dark Disney Central Casting. Hers was a life without Christmases; when she met and married my father, the most handsome, bravest and sweetest boy on the block in one of Bristol's many slum areas, Barton Hill (pronounced 'Bart Nil' in the Bristolian), all her Christmases came at once.

And what were her souvenirs of this shocking, once-in-a-lifetime win? Her wedding photographs, of course. And what did I, Demon Seed, do to her wedding photographs? Why, covered them in blue Biro scribble the minute I was old enough to hold a pen, of course. Clearly, my appetite for destruction was by now fully formed and there was no turning back.

I can't remember anything else really wicked from my pre-ado-lescence, apart from an inexplicable tendency to read the word 'friend' as 'fiend', leading to the memorable Sunday School inci-dent when I innocently asked if we could sing the lovely hymn 'What a Fiend We Have in Jesus' and was subsequently suspected of Wiccan tendencies. Perhaps this was a portent of things to come: 'There Are No Strangers, Only Fiends We Have Not Met'; 'Platonic Fiends'; 'A Fiend In Need Is A Fiend Indeed'; 'Fiends Are God's Apologies For Relations'; 'My Best Fiend's Girl'. Reader, I lived them all. Every one.

It was perhaps in my attitude to friendship, that sacred cow of the twentieth century, that I first displayed the germs of my sociopathy. Simply, I did not want them. Now, you can't say you don't want friends. You can say you don't want children. You can say you don't want a lover. You can say that you don't want a hus-band or wife. If you have aged, difficult parents you can show you don't want them by sticking them in a Home. ('Home', used as a place where unwanted old people are put, is one of the most sump-tuously hypocritical words of our time, I always think. A home is what they're already in. When they're turfed out by their ingrate issue, they're put into an anti-home, surely.)

But as we have broken free of the bonds of the family, we have wrapped ourselves senseless in the octopus of friendship instead; in many circles, the shedding of a friend is now considered far more shameful than the shedding of a spouse or a widowed, white-haired old mother. But from very early on in my life I never quite understood what friends were *for*. I could understand why people had people to do sex with or to do career with; these were arrange-ments of mutual beneficial exploitation and therefore made perfect sense. They seemed, as it were, organic; like a dog eating grass to make itself sick. But when it came to both friends and family, and the alleged wondrous glory of said relationships, I looked with the eyes of a child and saw little but sorrow.

Family first. Whenever the rising homicide rate agitates the population, some old liberal will step in and point out to us, the ignorant masses, chuckling comfortingly all the while, that the vast majority of murders take place within the family. So that's all right, then. Two women a week are currently being murdered by the man they live with and one child a week by its father or stepfather – but hey, the family that slays together stays together! When a girl swears 'Till death us do part', at least she has the reassurance of knowing that the architect of her death is more than likely standing right there with her before the altar, taking her life into his hands under the very eyes of God.

Why, for the love of Mike, it should be a comfort to us to know that our killer, should we be killed, will be a loved one is totally beyond me. And the grotesque selfishness of explaining to a homicide-fearing society that, hey, people generally only kill their own wives and infants so *you've* got nothing to worry about, Mr Jones, is surely the ultimate in the privatising of terror; all the stranger for usually coming from the liberal geek chorus of the penal-reform lobby. There is no such thing as society, indeed; kill your wife and get a caution because she nagged you or turned the football off, and the rest of society may sleep soundly in its bed.

Surely it is worse when people murder those they are supposed to be loving and caring for? Surely it is worse for a man to murder a sleeping wife or a crying child than it is for him to kill a fully grown, forewarned, possibly forearmed policeman? But no; even those who support capital punishment seem to think that domestic murders are nothing to write home about; that they are, in a way, natural. While such an assumption exists on the part of society it is hard not to conclude that, despite all the sugary, self-righteous cant about the Holy Family being the sacred bedrock of society, men generally have *carte blanche* to kill and maim, as they see fit, those who have the good luck to be related to them.

Because mine was such an atypical family – one child, working mother from as far back as I can remember, a father who while indubitably the head of the household was respected and recognized as such solely *because* of his singular qualities of gentleness and forbearance as against my mother's high-velocity bossiness – I had all the luxury of enjoying a stable childhood (as stable as a sociopath Martian was ever going to get, that is) while being able to observe the unhappiness of those more conventional families around me. And with very few exceptions, the families which had the expected 2.5 children, the mother at home and the father at large, seemed like end-of-the-pier, penny-in-the-slot tableaux of frozen domestic horror. One loving father kept hard-core pornography under his wardrobe; the next one was regularly raping his eight-year-old daughter, after finding out that she was being abused by an uncle and figuring that he might as well get some too, now that the seal was broken and the goods were damaged; another friend was being raped by her brother under fear of having her hamster put into the washing machine if she told. When it turned out that Charles Manson's small, sex-crazed, murderous unit was called 'The Family', people wondered why. I wondered why they wondered.

My father believed that, unless they were weak-minded or invalids, adults went mad if they did not have paid employment outside the home. Either that, or they committed adultery or turned seriously to drink, which my father saw as other, minor forms of insanity. In the few years my mother had stayed at home to mind me, she had become even more of a drama queen, vacillating between capering glee – usually with a garment, not a hat, on her head and her skirts gathered in one hand – or lumpen, sunken, armchair despair. When I was safely settled at Mixed Infants and a post at the local corner shop fell fallow my father dispatched her to it with some haste. I was five years old and the first latchkey child on my block; alas, my popularity was signed, sealed, delivered – and I wanted none of it.

Because already, at the age of five, in best sociopath tradition I was living inside my head. The dark, deep, lush interior of my tiny mind held a myriad of worlds, where there were monsters and I was a girl explorer, or where there was a future and I was middle class. Even then, though I don't know how, I was aware that in my neck of the woods AMBITION was a dirty word, from a foreign language, something dirtier and more shaming to the family honour than even something to do with S-E-X would be. The world turned and you grew up to do exactly, but *exactly*, as your parents had done before you, which in my case would mean a factory – preferably my mother's old alma mater of Mardon's, where I would make many a fine cardboard box until impregnated by a male of my class. I do not to this day understand how it got there, but I was already infected by a rogue gene which, without my five-year-old mind yet being able to express it, insisted that death would make a far better bridegroom.

And so, while still a Mixed Infant, I was insisting on an exacting and unusual price from the playmates who queued up to enjoy my after-school freedom with me, the freedom to burn Individual Bird's Eye Chicken Pies to a cinder and send my hamster (Happy by name, though knowing the twisted nature of extreme youth, probably not by inclination) for sedate spins on the hi-fi turntable at 33.3 r.p.m. (Don't tut, it could so easily have been the other way around.) *I was insisting that they pretend to be something they were not.*

For some reason, in the Nineteen Sixties in my part of Bristol in the county of Somerset, *no one pretended to be anything they weren't.* Not even the Mixed Infants. The truth was practised with the evangelical zeal and observance of minutiae of some new religion, carried to a quite pathological degree. What was it with these kids? Their parents cheated and lied like normal white folk, yet I do not once recall seeing my contemporaries step into the realm of fantasy long enough to play either Cowboys and Indians – rather, they simply fought – or Doctors and Nurses – rather, they simply gaped blankly at each other's genitalia.

Frankly, by the age of seven I felt like a case-worn therapist of deprived children, teaching my contemporaries step by weary step how simply to *play*:

'Now – Bridget/Karen/Jacqueline – the carpet's a swamp full of crocodiles. And the settee's our raft—'

'No iss not.' Stubborn little madam.

'No, listen – *pretend* it is!' Keep calm, Julie. Remember we're dealing with a revolutionary concept here: imagination.

'But iss *not*!'

Give me strength. 'Yes, but look – if you *pretend*—'

'But *why?*' Bridget/Karen/Jacqueline's frustration, as much a living, vibrant, tangible thing as is mine now, forces me to surrender the crocodile swamp affair. Let's try something nearer to my small, solitary heart.

'Look – let's do this instead. We're two girls, we're sixteen, we're living in a flat in London—'

'What – without our parents?' A sharp intake of breath from Bridget/Karen/Jacqueline.

'Well – *yes*. We're sixteen, and we share a flat—'

'But we're *not!*' The dumb, mute agony of the prosaic little brute is really quite horrible to behold; I give up, for the sake of both our mental healths.

But, despite my insane and much-mocked desire to pretend that things are not as they are, my popularity stays buoyant. I am puzzled by this. I can see the appeal; as a latchkey child, I live in the perfect state of virtual orphanhood that characterises all the best Blyton books from *Mallory Towers* to the *Famous Five* – all the security of a stable home life with none of the parental presence. My contemporaries, naturally enough, find this highly attractive. But when they gain entry to this magical kingdom, do they want to take advantage of this new-found freedom to 'do as thou wilt', as dirty old Aleister Crowley might put it? Do they, hell. They want to sit on the settee, drink Corona, watch *Magpie* and *crochet*.

Biding my time, I sit beside them and join them in the pastime of the moment a.k.a. crocheting a million tiny squares for God knows what greater purpose out of oddments of wool begged from our mothers or even, when we're desperate, secretly unpicking our own winter sweaters and hoping they'll have mysteriously grown back by the time they need to be worn again. If they haven't, I figure, I'll be all right; I'll *lie* about it, say the moths came with a S.W.A.T. squad. Though the dear knows what my imaginatively challenged little playmates will say.

But anyway, I bide my time and crochet another summer away. Who's to know that in my heart of hearts – that black little thing with the eyeless koala clinging to it – I feel like turning the single hooked pin on their smooth little throats and ripping out their innards?

It is the extreme *slowness* of my childhood days that stays with me – with all the sepia-tinted, Hovis-ad nostalgia of, say, shingles. That special shimmering slowness, that golden-syrup-poured-verrry-carefully-in-the-ear burr, that wading-waist-high-through-treacle, slurred, slow-motion sleep-walking that is singular to the West Country is, I can see now, uniquely attractive to a late-twentieth-century soul, jagged with sophistication, seeking the balm of end-less calm. At the time, however, twitching like a sticky little finger on the trigger of a gun, it drove me fucking mad.

West Country life was so slow, so very, very slow – even in a big Western city like Bristol – that on first seeing the famous motion picture *Invasion Of The Bodysnatchers* I found myself most per-plexed indeed. For it seemed to me at the time, where I came from, that the people were so docile, so conformist, so blank, that the pods would obviously have been the norm and the individual, quirky human beings immediately suspect as dangerous lunatics from another dimension.

Memoirs of working-class West Country life in the Nineteen Sixties are not so familiar that I can gallop away on my tale of a talented if trifling one-trick pony without first setting the scene. If we are talking about a memoir of a working-class West Country girl, then or at any other time, I can't think of one. The memoirs of a Cockney wide-boy; of an honest Northern lad – these have indeed been done to death. But the experiences of working-class English girls, from whatever region, rarely, if ever, see the light of day.

Fictionalized representations, even, of women of the modern working-class blood royal are also few, far between, and very fool-ish and dull indeed; they are the walking wounded who exist only to clip the wings of the yearning working-class boy in works of Northern realism. The allegedly 'Angry' (actually, examining the digestive and dipsomaniac history of John Osborne and his chums, more accurately dyspepsic, if the truth be told) Young Men of the

Fifties and Sixties (who I always felt would have benefited greatly from six months of National Service and a course of colonic irrigation, preferably at the same time) never saw their female counterparts as playmates or as co-conspirators in the great Outward Bound course of social counter-jumping, but rather as gooey, gluey honeypots who held you down while the system made mincemeat of you. In all the 'great' British films of the time, Laurence Harvey, Alan Bates and Albert Finney are time and time again prevented from going on to find a cure for cancer by getting June Ritchie, Shirley Anne Field or Rachel Roberts pregnant. And there was I thinking that it was (a) the savage and stifling socio-economic class system of this country and (b) their own quite surreal lack of ambition which held back young working-class men so very effectively.

Growing up, the experience of the Angry Young Men *vis-à-vis* the differing capabilities and desires of the proletarian genders was certainly not mine; maybe they put something in the Northern water which reverses the usual qualities of the sexes. I found young working-class men then to be almost uniformly some combination of the following winning character traits: crude, unimaginative, unattractive, thuggish, simple-minded, personally repellent. I do not remember ever having a crush on a single solitary one of them except, at the tender age of six, an exceptional and suitably named child called Kevin Sweet, whom I kissed, sweetly, in the cloakrooms most mornings, our mouths wide open and tongues probing in exact imitation of the Hollywood style, while my friend Jacqueline Dye stood right up next to us – practically with her head in our mouths – peering at our tiny undulating orifices, suckering at each other like twin pink sea anemones, and advising us, in the manner of Bernie the Bolt, 'Right a bit – left a bit—'. How such a state of affairs came about, for our infant kissing to be so meticulously and carpingly choreographed, I cannot for the life of me recall. But it seemed perfectly normal at the time; as most things, from eating dirt to being raped by your parents, apparently do to children, God help them.

But, Kevin Sweet apart, the male specimens I was surrounded

by were not, even at this dewy stage, anything to write home about – unless your father was a Right-wing eugenics merchant intent on proving the generic vileness of the young post-war working-class male child, that is. It remains a hard fact of life to this very day that between working-class young males and females there appears to be a massive gap in everything from physical beauty to finer feelings. And this is why I find it so puzzling that the plight of the working-class male has so often been the subject of art, while that of his female contemporary has been all but ignored. Once we have taken into account Shelagh Delaney's *A Taste Of Honey* and Barbara Windsor's *Laughter And Tears Of A Cockney Sparrer*, we are The Invisible. And if there is any higher message than 'Gimmee' behind this book, I hope it is to provide proof that we, The Invisible, lived and died as lividly as anyone else.

And we were, I believe, worth much more than most. Because I am convinced that, at her best, the young working-class woman is perhaps the ultimate evolutionary point of the human species, whether we are looking for beauty, sensitivity or compassion. It is perhaps because we are so superior to the rest of mankind, between the ages of twelve and twenty-four, that mankind perseveres so relentlessly in his attempts to make us appear silly, shallow figures of ridicule and attacks us – sexually, intellectually, physically – in every way he can, to wipe out our living testimony to his own bestiality and ugliness.

A great feminist writer of antiquity once remarked that 'women have no idea how much men hate them'. Great though she was, the fact that she was both Australian and bourgeois banned her from the state of grace that young working-class Englishwomen bathe in for the formative years of their lives. Had she had this benefit, she would be aware that long before men loathe women, women loathe men. Or rather, before they are wilfully and disgustingly whipped to a state of frothing hormonal frenzy by the secret agents of socialization, girls hate boys.

That the sexes have very little in common when not actually horizontal, ballroom dancing or engaged in the due process of revolution, and that girls are repelled and disgusted by boys the moment their tiny eyes can distinguish pink from blue, can be seen as soon as boys and girls begin to walk and long before they can talk. A million studies of infants playing under the eye of a hidden camera have noted that while infant girls are instinctively attracted to each other and, once having established contact, go out of their tiny way generally to co-operate and make life nicer for each other in any little way their minute minds can grasp, boy babies will first attempt to bash the living daylights out of each other (or better still, a girl) and then, when restrained, 'play' with another tot only within the very loosest definitions of the word, preferably using it whenever possible as a piece of non-sentient matter over which to drive miniature trucks, into which to hammer large plastic nails and so on. And, though the trucks and nails may cease being tools of play and become the real McCoy, these patterns of rest and recreation pretty much remain, especially in the working-class lad not unmanned by book learning.

By the time she is of school age, on the other hand, the average working-class girl-child will have been drilled rigorously in the daintiest manners this side of Tara and will observe personal hygiene to within an inch of her pristine little life. She may well be wearing that modern monstrosity a 'trainer' bra, and if Boots the Chemist could only be persuaded to stock them would be almost certainly, under the aegis of her bodyphobic mother (made bodyphobic over several decades of unsatisfactory sexual mauling by males, needless to say), be stuffing 'trainer' tampons up her tiny twat. Cleanliness is not just next to Godliness to the young girl; it is her very religion. At this precious stage, too tender to touch, too contemptuous to cower, every little girl is an Estella, radiant with her own piqued purity.

Boys, insofar as she ever thinks of them, head to silky Silvikrin head with her equally sweet-smelling eight-year-old Best Friend – probably called Jessica, as best friends, bridesmaids, but, strangely, rarely brides inevitably are – shell-pink mouths making delicious little moues of disgust, are not just a sex but a species apart. More than a species, in fact, for little girls love fluffy pussy-cats, satin-eared pups and suedey, snooty ponies. More than anything else on earth, including semi-precious gemstones and Mongolian grandmothers, boys are simply *other*. The smelling, the yelling, the uncultured-vulture torturing, the sheer *vileness* of them!

And then what happens? In an act of unparalleled cruelty and illogicality, the supreme rude awakening takes place. Having raised their little princess to believe that she must never touch herself 'down there' except for the express purpose of keeping it cleaner than a communion chalice, that it is in fact a Holy of Holies, the dainty creature is then suddenly informed, with no warning but with truly awesome diagrams, that it is her biological destiny to be slobbered over by a chosen one of the dreaded nose-picking, bum-scratching, seat-sniffing tribe of trolls, after which she will be held down and sweated upon until he has managed to squirt a goodly wad of off-white slime inside her. And for this she has been glossed, flossed, scented and silkened to a state of unearthly perfection over a period of some sixteen years! No wonder they have to dress the abomination up with an ocean of white tulle and a dirty great cake with which to stuff the blushing bride insensible! And they wonder why women are putting off marriage longer and longer. The minute they *could*, of course they *would*!

Think about it. When you look at a wedding it looks lovely, doesn't it? The beautiful bride in her beautiful dress. The less beautiful bridesmaids in their less beautiful dresses. The dog of a matron of honour in a dress that only a mother-in-law bent on making a fool of a girl could love. A field of living, breathing, parti-coloured flowers, moving on swaying stalks towards the benediction of their own beauty.

And then, who's this? The ugly pug in the dark, ill-fitting suit, sweating from last night's best man's blowjob, his mouth still sour from performing cunnilingus on a syphilitic stripper? Why, it's the bridegroom – ready, willing and hopefully able to violate an angel on her big day. That's why women are putting off marriage for as long as they can – because every wedding has to have a bridegroom. If there were two brides there would be a mad stampede to Pronuptia. The bridegroom is indeed the mourner at every wedding.

It's Alive!

So this is what the long, slow summer of my West Country working-class girlhood is inevitably building up to: death by matrimony. Even as a tot, I just *know* it. And walking across the high wire from childhood to well-adjusted adolescence I will trip, totter and fall off.

And I will fly.

CHAPTER TWO

My Life
as a Dog

I grew up in the dappled Dralon springtime of twentieth century
British social history; between the black and white marge-scraping
years of post-war re-grouping and the come-on-down Sen-
surround of the Thatcher era. It was neither the best of times nor
the worst, but it was well and truly modern. Suddenly everyone
came from nowhere and knew nothing. We were born-again
babies, all of us, scampering happily in the plush playpen of con-
sumerism. I liked it a *lot*.

Mr Macmillan, Prime Minister between the years of 1957 and
1964, oversaw my infancy like a benign walrus. Truly I had never
had it so good. *But then, neither had the world, heh heh!* Because it
had never had *me* before.

Despite the tranquillity of my parents' marriage, it was very easy
to feel a thing in freefall, without recourse to any true roots or tradition. This suited me just fine. The Bristol Sound – as Portishead
would later demonstrate with their almost unbearably beautiful
music – is the sound of sleep-walking, of a region which has his-
torically been left, for good or ill, out of the North–South debate,
which has been forgotten except for the annual escape to the
beauty spots of the West. Affluent from trading, unmarked and
uneducated by the sense of great wrongs done for the love of
money which has moulded working-class thought in other parts of

the country from Wales to Walsall, neither did we have the ill-humoured, inbred isolationism which affects the deep West such as Cornwall. We didn't *think* about anywhere else enough to feel resentful. Growing up there, I felt totally isolated; an island on an island.

Nothing made sense from as far back as I can remember; nothing I ever experienced referred back to anything else which could be really proved to be 'real'. My life was as surreal, yet as seemingly banal, as a fishcake, from the word go. Professor Roger Scruton would later write that I had had at some point (artfully unspecified) to kill Julie Burchill in order to become 'Julie Burchill', but looking at my own lack of continuity I wonder if the one unprotected by the armour of the inverted ever really existed at all. It was a time in history when there was no history. When everything was hire purchase – buy now and pay later, live now and pay later. And I couldn't imagine any better way.

My father called himself a Communist, but so far as I could tell, very early on he was actually a Soviet patriot born on the wrong patch of soil. Admiration for the Soviet Union was widespread among the adults I grew up around in the late Sixties and early Seventies; not for any idealistic reasons, but because whereas our government was seen as soft, the Soviets were seen as admirably hard. 'The Russians would 'ave them sorted out in five minutes!' was the saloon-bar cry that met most political problems: the situation in Ireland, in the Middle East, in the streets of the black neighbourhoods of our own country. Aberfan, even. They stopped short only of swearing that the Russians would sort out the trades unions, who were busily engaged in preparing to Hold The Country To Ransom.

My father, as luck would have it, did not therefore have his loyalty to the Soviet Union brought into the balance. For he was about to embark upon his union career, working unpaid for the Union of Shop, Distributive and Allied Workers. For as long as I could remember I had thought that 'Capitalist!' – never heard without at least one exclamation mark – was a swear-word, like bastard, of the very first fetid water. Now, with the official mantle of a union covering his broad shoulders, he was ready to put his agitation into practice.

It makes me laugh when the soft Left get cross at the Right for saying that the trades unions were run by a bunch of Communists in the 1970s. Of course the grim grandees at the very top – Murray, Feather, Gormley – were house-trained. They even seemed to believe that they were tenants. But below them, moving through the body politic of Seventies Britain with the stealth and malice of a beautiful virus, most men who were involved in trade unionism *were* Communists and were sympathetic to the Soviet Union. Which is just as it should be.

I will never understand why it is acceptable for Right-wing Britons to genuflect, crawl and generally suck ass to the United States, while it was supposed to be a sin for Left-wing Britons to behave even civilly to the Soviet Union. As we now can see – especially, ironically, the Right-wing, virulently anti-Communist newspapers such as the *Daily Mail* – America has actually inflicted much more damage on this country than the Soviet Union would ever have dreamed of. All the things the Right hates about contemporary British society are nasty habits we have picked up from America – fast food, guns, AIDS, wearing your hat the wrong way round. True, the Soviet Union might have felt the need to shoot a few writers and the Royal Family if they had ever invaded us (which they had, of course, never once desired to do). But who can put hand on heart and say that this fair isle would not be a finer place without Prince Philip and Jeffrey Archer? Not I, sociopath, in all honesty.

So we were in effect a Communist household. We were the enemy within. But because working-class British people have never ever been scared of Socialism, rather in fact seeing it as the norm – and Tony Blair's unique evil is that he, a Labour Party leader, has sought to make Socialism as frightening a word in this country as it is in America, that while every vox pop shows the welfare state to be practically the *religion* of the British he has relentlessly ploughed on with his lunatic Sunday School Capitalism – even the most conformist of neighbours in our extremely conformist neighbourhood never raised an eyebrow. The woman up the road who had eyes of two different colours (one hazel, one green) was tut-tutted about – but never my father the Communist.

Also – and here is my first Handy Pre-Millennial Household Hint, of which there will be several – nothing works as well when it comes to getting rid of cold-calling, door-stepping Mormons and Jehovah's Witnesses as saying casually, 'Sorry, we're Communists here.' If you really want to traumatise them, be sure to follow this up with 'Wait! – come in and have a cup of tea (which they're not allowed to drink, in case it turns them into ravening beasts), I'd love to talk to you about the Soviet way', as they scamper back whence they came at a rate of knots. If you can't be bothered, a brief 'We're Jews' is just as, if not more, frightening to these strange and strangulated salvation salesmen, who obviously, without meaning to be judgemental, don't know the first fucking thing about God in all his might and majesty, or they wouldn't go around attempting to flog him on people's doorsteps as though he were a Dust Devil. This, too, is an American import, and easily as delightful as a bucket of McNuggets swallowed whole without liquid, or a drive-by shooting for the sake of a pair of running shoes.

We were thrilled the day the telephone arrived. This was in the Sixties and we were profoundly working class, so it was like a yacht, say, would be to you people out there, whom, just between you, me and the doorpost I'll always, deep down, despise unless you started from prole position too, because that's just the way things are. Fish gotta swim, birds gotta fly and the smart money says that if you're not from where I'm from I'll never respect you. I have definitely loved people who weren't working class – but I could never *respect* one. God, no! It would be as silly and inappropriate as pledging one's troth to a fish finger. Not that I don't *like* fish fingers. But I couldn't consider one of them my equal. I suppose this is what they call a ghetto mentality. Ooo, I *like* it like that!

I sat on the stairs and stared at the phone as my father showed my mother how to work it. The Union would pay the bills, apparently. And it was a red telephone, which surely was most unusual? I wondered if in some way these two facts were connected. Could it be, literally, a hot-line to Moscow? I shivered. I hoped so. I had already decided that, if 'gusset' was the ugliest word in the world (followed closely by 'spasm' and 'crust') then 'sabotage' was the most beautiful. I've always been up for a spot of sabotage, and consider it to this day to be perhaps the most undervalued of all the black arts. Was this, in fact, the very telephone on which the call would come from Moscow telling us to Hold The Country To Ransom once and for all?

My mother has other plans, I can already tell, as she keeps insisting stubbornly that ooo, Bill, she *still* isn't sure she can do it, and show me again. My mother, as has been mentioned, is one extremely strong-willed diva, the Carmen of the cardboard box, the Tosca of the tea-break, the very Medea of Mardon's, Son and Hall, in fact. But feminism is still such a non-specifically scary word that she feels the occasional need to play the Helpless Little Lady – not easy when you're five foot ten with eyes like angry blue police lights and hands all but permanently clenched into fists, all the better to jump over the garden fence and brawl with the neighbour lady with. And actually, the word 'feminism' is still putting resin on its *pointe* shoes in the wings of the future; it's called 'Women's Lib' in the Sixties and Seventies – which now sounds distressingly like some sort of sanitary protection forced upon us by the gravelly, blood-clot aural intimacies of Claire Rayner – and begins and ends with one desire: to 'burn yer bra'. The fact that buying a box of matches is already an established right – even for unmarried women – seems to be beyond the mental grasp of that small and sad segment of any given male population who are so insecure in their own manhood that they suffer from a positively eye-rolling, erection-losing fear of female equal rights in any shape or form. In my opinion, a man is a Man if he is good at sex. If he is, he won't be thrown into a tizzy by feminism, ever. Because he knows where his manhood resides and it's something no woman will *ever* have (unless she has an operation and even then it won't work anything like as well as his). A man who can only define himself as a Man because a woman is a slave is no Man at all, but a piping, spiteful castrato.

But anyway, like the massive majority of strong women of her class, my mother would rather break rocks in the hot sun – with her forehead – than *admit* to being a 'strong woman'. To this day, I too find it a singularly squirmy phrase. It seems to me that whenever a man calls a woman 'strong', he is justifying why he has done or is about to do something *really nasty* to her. I once read an essay by the brilliant black American feminist writer Michelle Wallace, in which at the height of the Black Is Beautiful thang she was watching a television documentary on black American poverty. A woman was shown, worn out before thirty, living in gut-wrenching poverty, bringing up half a dozen children by different men who had not deigned to stick around long enough to see them cut their milk teeth. She seemed utterly and understandably defeated by her life. The Black Power dude sitting next to Ms Wallace shook his head solemnly and whistled through his teeth: 'That is one *strong* sister.' 'Strong woman', used by men, means 'she can take it'. And if she can take it, why not do it to her again?

When used by women themselves, the phrase is less offensive but more risible. Strong women, like my mother and others of her class, who have grown up in real hardship, then gone on in the second round to bring up their children and earn a living, whether or not they are married, *as a matter of course* – no 'career or children' crap for working-class women; they have *always* worked, and expected to, for the simple reason that they know, despite their lack of formal education, that they are not retards, children or cripples, so why on earth should they want to live their one and only life as a parasite? – never refer to themselves as such.

This privilege, it seems to me, is reserved almost exclusively for women who toil in the salt mines of showbusiness, dragging themselves on hands and knees between the merciless heat of the Klieg lights and the arid wastes of the Hospitality Suite, accompanied on their lonely, endless travails only by three children, two nannies, a stylist, an agent, a male secretary, a PA and a partridge in a pear tree (virtually fat free, natch). They are 'strong women'. (To make matters even more delicious, Neneh Cherry has a daughter – a *daughter* – called Tyson. Imagine the exchange in ten years' time: 'Mummy, who was I named after?' 'You were named after a man whose job it was to dish out brain damage to his fellow black men in public for a great deal of money and for the savage, para-sexual amusement of rich white people, darling. And whose idea of fun was to beat up and rape black women.' 'Oh. Thanks, Mum.') And faced with the smorgasbord of totally unjustified self-adoration which they trail in their wake like a really noxious perfume – say Poison – you too will need to be strong. Or at least, to have a strong stomach, *to keep from throwing up*. Heh heh heh!

Personally, I believe that the phrase 'strong woman' should be reserved for those awesome ladies who appear in the Olympic Games shotting the putt and all that. Or ladies in travelling fairs and freak shows who lift huge weights. You're not a strong woman if you're simply a showbiz slapper who has undergone the perfectly ordinary process of gestation and childbirth and then had a sit-com script accepted by BBC2. You're a strong woman if you can lift a huge dumb-bell with a skimpily clad blonde sitting on either end.

But nevertheless, my mother is a toughie, who doesn't want to be seen as a bossyboots wife. Worshipping my dad as she does, she couldn't bear it if he were ever considered to be – God forbid! – henpecked in the eyes of the neighbours. Not being as smart as me, of course, she doesn't realise that this could simply never happen. Because my father (Leo, wouldn't you know it) possesses such natural gravitas and confidence and Gary Cooper masculinity – as opposed to John Wayne masculinity, which is hysterical and neurotic, and signifies that you probably wear puce lace camiknickers under your khakis – that if he were to walk up the main drag wearing a tutu, a pointed dunce's hat, curling vari-coloured jester slippers with bells on the toes and all the while pushing a chihuahua dressed up as a baby in a pram, the neighbour ladies would *still* swoon so breathily that their lace curtains would shimmer in the breeze, and they'd swoon 'Ooo! There goes Bill Burchill. They broke the mould, they did, when they made him. *Such* a gentle-man. In the *real* meaning of the word. A gentle man. But so strong . . . a gentle giant . . .'

But my mum isn't quite aware of the total respect my dad has in the hood: Gandhi and Gary Cooper rolled into one. She just figures he's your common-or-garden deity type, so once in a while she'll throw this helpless act which fools no one, least of all my father. She'll pretend she can't cross roads, and purposely run off into the teeming traffic so my father has to chase her and rescue her (in the process putting his life in danger, but, hey, it's one way of proving your love). Or after half a Snowball (a senseless concoction of lemonade and advocaat – devil's advocaat, to judge by the dis-gusting colour, taste and texture) she'll suddenly say, apropos of nothing, that she hopes she goes first. Dies, she means. Really! Talk about bringing the party down!

'Ooo, Bill! I *can't*!' As patient as history, my father demonstrates one more time how to dial numbers. I catch his eye and he shakes his head. My snicker is stillborn in my throat and I slink upstairs to my bedroom.

Prince growls, with no malice but merely from habit, as I pass him where he lazes on the landing.

'Oh, piss off, Prince!'

He realizes it's me and gapes at me amiably. It's only my mother he hates. It's only her he prevents from using the toilet when my father is sleeping, which he does in the daytime because he now works the nightshift. My mother isn't allowed to use the toilet because it's upstairs, as toilets usually are, and of course upstairs is where my father sleeps. And where my father sleeps, naturally Prince will lie across the threshold of that room, snarling.

If my father's natural authority works a treat on people, then it is very catnip to dogs. In the presence of my father all dogs instantly become Old Shep, willing to toss themselves into a watery maelstrom death to rescue him, to cross continents to be with him, to terrorise his wife to guarantee his slumber. My dad is the reason dogs were first created. He *is* the reason why dogs are loyal to the point of hara-kiri. If dogs truly are a man's best friend, my dad was the man God had in mind when he created dog. Forget woman. If God had taken a rib from Adam and created dog instead, most men would never have noticed her missing. And it would have saved a whole lot of trouble.

The dog my dad has today (who was for some curious reason, best not thought about for too long, already named Benito when they got him; naturally this has been shortened to Benny, my Red Dad is damned if he's going to let the neighbours think he's gone mad and is calling to the restless spirit of Mussolini each evening) is a small, sweet-natured mongrel. But even this little fellow, so sunny that he is practically a huge wagging tail with a bit of dog attached, like one of those weird ferret-on-a-ball toys, has it bad for my dad. My dad's dogs love him so much, in fact, that they end up all but stalking him. In his own home! This Benny, for instance: the moment my dad leaves the room he hyperventilates. We have to give him a brown paper bag to breathe deeply into. My dad now finds it easier to let Benny follow him everywhere – the bathroom, the toilet, the pub.

Our dogs aren't called Prince any more. But they used to be. My dad started keeping dogs as a teenager. There was Black Prince, a black (surprise) Labrador, and then Golden Prince, a Labrador of precious hue. Then came the real Prince and after that they broke the mould. Or rather, Prince probably attacked it, snarling, and mauled it to bits. That's the kind of guy he was.

Prince was an Alsatian by birth – a German Shepherd dog, this breed is also called. We didn't like the Germans in our house, in common with most people not working twenty-four hours a day at being Sensitive Human Beings, so that was Rule One he broke for a start.

Then there was the delicate issue of 'The Kiddie' (*Moi*). Prince showed himself very soon to be a premature practitioner of the holistic health philosophy, i.e. listen to your body because your body knows what it wants. What Prince's body wanted, it seemed, quite early on in his career as a barker, was human flesh.

My father came from a family of four brothers and one sister, the eldest of them being George. George was a bit on the posh side:

lived in a detached house; white collar; got divorced from a vampy first wife and married an up-market mystery called Connie. At Christmas, when the extended family drunkenly wassailed from one of the Burchill houses to another, Connie was the only greeter to sit us all down, feed us coffee and make us play pen-and-paper games. The adults went along with it, because they were adults, but my cousins Kim and Mark and I were invariably dumbstruck by her impudence. From the age of nine, we looked forward to getting totally blitzed on vodka and lime at Christmas. It was as traditional as satsumas, stuffing and sicking up the said. The Burchill brothers tolerated Connie's dainty ways for many years, but relations were finally severed when she presented the fourteen-year-old Kim with a salt cellar – one, 1 – for Christmas.

Anyway, George it was, with typical lack of street smarts, who used to gurn at, cross his eyes at, thumb his nose at and generally taunt Prince through the glass of the front-room window whenever his insurance selling brought him to Brislington (*not* the Islington of Bristol, incidentally; more like the White City) before formally announcing his visit by ringing the doorbell in the usual way. I used to sit on the lounge sofa in my Pod and watch George tormenting the by now frenzied beast – a dirty great drooling psychopath with a leg at each corner, if the truth be told, which it certainly wasn't in any way, shape or form about Prince in our house – and wonder why grown-ups were so stupid. I knew one day Prince would 'ave 'im.

My Pod, it seemed to me at the time, was an actual if invisible Pod which I surrounded myself with simply by reading for many hours on end, until I was completely cut off from my physical surroundings. I've known lots of people who read lots of books, but I've never met anyone who read the way I read as a child. I would read books not just industri*ously* – Bristol City coat of arms: VIRTUTE ET INDUSTRIA, which made many a young boy or girl snicker when I told them it, while lying in their bed at 3 p.m. on a working day after performing some unspeakable feat of filth upon them – but industri*ally*, like a machine processing paper. Every Saturday morning, and after school on Wednesdays, I would trot urgently to Sandy Park Library suffering that swirling liquid-silk excitement in my stomach which only comes in adult life at the prospect of seeing a loved one. And I *was* anticipating seeing a loved one. One million loved ones. *Books.*

Books were everything to me as a child. Long before pop music saved my life, books did. Before I even considered suicide, books saved my life by removing me from existence. Books helped me *save my life up*, squirrel it away like something precious for a rainy day, while my body performed the outward motions of the doomed-to-disappointment working-class girl-child. When people want to indicate that they read a lot – 'voraciously', if you want me to spew – as children, they always say, 'I would even read the cereal packet'. How pathetically stupid. Why, when they could have read a book? And all cereal packets say the same thing: NOW WITH ADDED FIBRE! FREE! ROSIE AND JIM TRANSFER INSIDE! It's hardly Proust, is it?

Neither were the books I read. They were better. They were about gymkhanas (mostly Pat Smythe's feisty 'Jill' books), boarding schools (*Mallory Towers* was top) and best of all ballet schools – Lorna Hill's singularly inspired Sadler's Wells books. They were about perfect worlds; about girls unhampered by either parents or boys and thus free to be themselves, perfectly girls. Despite the routine dismissal of such juvenile *fumetti* as mindless pulp, there is more female aspiration, determination and sheer *character* in one Wells book than in the entire oeuvre of Anita Brookner. A girl is a woman who has not yet been house-trained by the heavy hand, by the long arm of the law of her womb.

So I would enter that library – a real, proper library in the Sixties, no leaflets or videos or Community Billboard, not even any paperbacks – as silently as a supplicant seeking salvation and leave like a prancing pony all set to carry his blushing bride across the threshold, to *break her spine* with my hot little hands. All four spines: from very early on, I went in for group text. I'd get those babies home, put them in a pile on the table in front of me and I'd go for it; one chapter from each, in strict rotation. At first reading at normal speed, I would soon rev up and almost *attack* the poor quartet, like a page-cutting machine. I would read myself into a frenzy of bliss.

Sometimes my mother would come into the room, watch me silently for a few moments and start crying. I noticed early on that my reading had the power to upset people. My mother thought it meant I was a mass murderer in the making – they were notoriously 'loners', after all – or, even worse, that I was *unpopular*. To the working-class mothers of daughters, this is a worse prospect than having their darling daughter marry a leper or a leprechaun, so long as he's in work.

My mother would burst into tears and gesture at the street. If it was a weekend you'd see girls going past in pairs. Not snogging or on their way to a riot or anything, just being boring, best done in pairs. 'I'm sick of it!' she'd sob. 'Girls together all the time!' (Kinky! Let's hope I made her happy when I did a runner with Charlotte R) 'And you'm in 'ere . . . *reading*!' She would fling herself against the wall, weeping, and I would look at her curiously for a moment before gathering up my four books, leaving the room and resuming my Edward Scissorhands routine in the back parlour. Often, if she had nothing better to do, she'd follow me from room to room persecuting me until I took residence in the toilet, still calmly rote-reading on. I couldn't be touched when I was in the hands of a book.

I was by now well established in my mother's mind as an antisocial reader, who cruelly used reading as a weapon. At the age of four, I'd actually been removed from my nursery school because of my adorable habit of waking up the other children during their nap hour, marching from bed to tiny bed reading aloud to them. Some of the wusses ended up crying because their sleep had been disturbed. I ask you! What was it about my reading that made people start crying? And didn't they see how much more attractive that made it?

I'd seen girls going about in poxy pairs, anyway, and I thought they were pathetic. The things that passed for fun! Worse, I considered several of these pairings *evil*. Yes, I'd actually experienced evil at first hand by the age of ten. I was in the library one Saturday morning when the uncouth snickering of two of my class-mates, Susan and Georgina by name, drew my attention. I was surprised, to say the least, to see Susan and Georgina inside *my* library. Saturday mornings were when all the uncouth girls gathered 'down town', haunting the cosmetic counters of Woolworths and Boots like tarty ghosts, blowing their pocket money on Miners Face Shapers, which they slashed on in great stripes of pearlised white and glossy plum, making themselves look like Red Indians in full war paint (see mid-period Adam Ant for a demonstration of how *not* to apply face shader), and Cutex nail polish in extremely pale and pearly tints, which made them look as though they were undergoing cardiac arrest.

In fact, I couldn't have wished anything better on 'Sue' and 'George' as they staggered sniggering over to me, clutching each other like drowning men hell-bent on winning a three-legged race. 'Oi! Ju!' God! The ignominy! I looked around guiltily. Ju! Which came out as *Jew*! Which I certainly wasn't, not even by injection yet. But what if other people thought I was one? And that Sue and George were anti-Semites? And that I was now expected to associate with them?

Oblivious to my disgust and loathing – probably because I was simpering like a madman; Sue and George were the two most popular girls in my year, after all, and my mother's brainwashing had had some superficial effect, if nothing more – they staggered over. Sue wanted the lavatory and – wouldn't you know it – George quickly espied a copy of the children's classic *The World of Pooh* by Mr A. A. Milne. Much mirth resulted before Sue and George dragged me from my haven in order to trawl the local shopping precinct. Outside the library their glee grew until they were barely able to stand. I did not know why until George pulled a book from her crocheted 'squatter' bag. A *library book*! But George couldn't possibly have a library ticket, let alone *four* like me. She was the only girl in our class to read 'Cathy & Claire' with her lips, hips and Kirbygrips moving. So she had removed the book *without a stamp*! I gaped at the pair in astonishment.

By now I had promised my soul to Satan if I could have sex with

Marc Bolan before I started menstruating, drawn pentangles and smoked aspirin to summon up Beezlebub himself as some sort of fiendish dating-bureau chief wallah ('For the discerning professional and diabolical person *exclusively*'). Marc Bolan, he of the corkscrew curls, perfect cheek bones and quite singular degree of self-love, which must have made it extremely advisable for him to wear condoms during masturbation lest he get himself pregnant, was *the* first big passion of my pubescent fantasy life, who gave me the ultimate just-what-I've-always-wanted gift of lust. (A gift I am to acknowledge with exquisite grace and gratitude in later life when, a week before his death, he gently approaches my seventeen-year-old self in the Roxy Club and asks if he may buy me a drink. I, so lividly young, pale and thin, engraved on life with all the insight and compassion of a scar, sneer and turn away because he is old, fat and past it. Never meet your heroes; not because they will let you down, but because *you* will betray *them*. Judas was the first fan.)

So anyway; girls are supposed to go from ponies to boys. But they don't; they go from ponies to *black magic* to boys. When we were ten, ouija boards were passing hands behind raised desks like pornography, pot and Pamela Anderson's phone number rolled into one in an all-boy boarding-school. And perhaps the black magic is a last desperate attempt to stave off the slavery of full-on joyless heterosexuality. Because you might as well sell your soul to Satan if it's going to be slowly but surely destroyed by marriage to some man anyway.

The point is that I considered myself a kiddie of Crowley, a sister of de Sade, a concubine of Tommy Cooper – basically an all-round in-law of inversion despite the glaringly obvious fact that I was, to all intents and purposes, a ten-year-old virgin who religiously, and that is both literal and metaphorical, thanked God for her intact state every day because if Plan A (sleeping with Marc before menstruation and so selling soul to aforesaid Satan) failed then Plan B was to become a nun, and no messing. The point is, I knew I was *bad*.

But now, here, in the slumberous suburban Saturday, I stare

into the abyss. Because *not only have Sue and George removed a library book without a stamp – they are now tearing pages from it, laughing like larceny and casting them to the wind! A book! Like dust in the wind!* George looks at me and holds out the book, and her beautiful brown eyes are warm with genuine fellowship. Never believe that the bad do not feel fellowship. They do – more than others. 'Have a go?'

Here it is. My chance to enter the In Crowd. Make my mother happy. Glide through my teens like an ice-dancer to a perfect ten finish. Never be assaulted, bullied, cornered. Simple as ABC. So I grab the book, hold it to the place where my breasts will one day keep their appointment with sexual destiny, draw myself up to my full height, pull my lips back over my teeth and literally *howl* at the arbiters of my social destruction: 'You! And you! *Fuck off!*'

It is the first time I have ever spoken the F-word. I must seem mad. Sue and George run for it. I stand there on the street, sobbing very quietly, holding the book to my body, hoping in some vague way to feed it back to health as books have forever fed me into some semblance of sentience. I squeeze it. It feels thin. I know it is already dead. I lay it gently on the library steps. I don't even bother to look at the title. All I know is that a book is dead. 'Fuck. Oh, *fuck.*' And I cry.

It was probably a Barbara Cartland.

George shouldn't have tormented me. She made me do it. And George, my father's elder brother, shouldn't have tormented Prince.

From my mother I got my fire, always up for a bit of needless if necessary violence. From my father I got my ice. So many times he and I have watched George making faces at Prince through the window. We've never said anything about it, to each other or to George. But we've looked at each other, with the stolid acceptance of the only two people in the world who believe that State Capitalism is not a stage which must be passed through on the way to Communism proper, but actually *better*, if you think about it sensibly. We know we will bury them. And we know that Prince will bite George.

The 'Kiddie' issue. When I was waiting to be born, my time come round at last, the swift death of Prince was advocated on all sides. He was, after all, an Alsatian; Alsatians, like Asians, were considered, in the Fifties, a dreadful threat to the general quiet, while they are now revered as pillars of society and often held up to make pitbulls and Anglo-Caribbeans look bad. But my dad wouldn't have it. He knew best. He had the tiny pond in the garden filled in and closed up. He had fire guards which looked like massive medieval iron masks mounted around each electric bar. He stayed a Communist, through Hungary, when the last gasp of Fascism was routed by the reviled, radiant Red Army of the Russians. He did everything to make the world safe and shiny for his baby girl. But the Prince must not die.

When my father opened the front door to his brother that day – the brother who wasn't working class any more, the brother who wore a white collar and married more than once – he failed to close the door that could separate Prince from his tormentor. As the beast bounded towards his disrespectful repast I recalled the way Prince had treated me, against all odds and Cassandras. The time when, as a five-year-old, I had taken toothpaste and a brush to his teeth, shoving both far down his throat, and he had lain there in the hallway wide awake and uncomplaining while my parents, stumbling upon us well into the grooming, looked on in awe and pride. The times I had ridden thoughtlessly upon his noble back, thrashing his rump as one would a horse, and he had lowered his lovely alarming head and reserved his better judgement.

The time when somehow, from somewhere, Prince, a dog, made some sort of moral decision. And when my father, one night, came after me up the stairs on all fours in the context of a chase game, Prince, sitting in endless censure at the top of the stairs, saw me run past him screaming. And when my father, his final love, his idol, the very consideration on his heart, presumed to pass Prince in pursuit, Prince just . . . *hauled off.* And for the first and last time, Prince barred my father's way, his mouth a snarling Stonehenge; the little brat who'd brushed his teeth and bruised his tush, somehow, by stealth of hand, without them seeing, his everything.

35

Stealing loyalty: perhaps the ultimate peacetime thrill. My father didn't make a sound; didn't ever make a sound. Just smiled at me, above it all. He looked the same when Prince put the world to rights with George. When Russia put the world to rights with Fascist Hungary.

'Daddy, my daddy!' Jenny Agutter's cry in the last frame of *The Railway Children* summed up all the inarticulate, agonising, utterly sexless adoration a girl should have the right to feel for her father. Strong, long, silent, non-violent and as mysterious as a mermaid, my father not only gave me life but saved my life with his endless example of just how sweet and strong a man could be.

It was the last day of junior school. That afternoon I breezed into the house. 'Dad!' He was on nights, so he'd be up, having break-fast at four. He came towards me. He looked so big. He was so quiet. I saw him silhouetted in the hallway. I felt my world spin and I knew that I was about to become an adult. 'Dad . . . we had a conjuror . . .'

'Prince is dead.'

I went up to him, a thin blonde girl of eleven, and took him, my gentle giant, my Gary Cooper, in my arms. He cried, for the only time.

'Sssh.' I patted his back. As his tears fell on me, I felt baptised by the benediction of the ultimate Best Man. I shivered, and a rictus smile swept my lips, despite myself. Now nothing could stop me.

I'll cry at anything. Apparently this is a sign of sociopathy; people say that to me who don't cry much. But I prefer to think that it might be a sign of someone who genuinely feels empathy with other people. Having said that, I believe that, as a rule, only women should cry. God knows we've got enough reasons to! When it comes to men I tend to subscribe to the line: 'Beware of the man who cries; he cries only for himself.'

Things Women are Allowed to Cry at
• Childbirth

- Weddings
- Death, especially of fictional characters on television
- Pet Rescue
- When drunk, anything
- Looking at old photographs
- Playing records by depressed black women, especially 'Stay With Me Baby'
- The 'Lilibolero' on the World Service
- Sunsets
- Last Night of the Proms
- One-night stands
- After sex
- During sex
- Before periods
- Your man done you wrong
- Torn between two lovers
- 'You've never been to You'
- 'Unchained Melody'

Things Men are Allowed to Cry at
- VE Day
- VJ Night
- The dog dying

Somewhere towards the end of the Sixties and the start of the Seventies – that shimmering, sunlit time when the moral freedom of one decade bore material fruit in another – my parents started going to Butlin's, Bognor Regis, for their annual holiday. We'd never gone without before – the Isle of Wight (when I was sick on the boat), Paignton (when I was sick on the train) and Mevagissey (when I was sick on the dog) all hold fond, if fetid memories. But for an imaginative, hedonistic, working-class, girl-child on the Sixties–Seventies cusp when all seemed briefly possible, Butlin's was indeed very heaven. Hog heaven. Hog wild. Wild mouse. It was every sort of thrill, all come at once. For me, it truly was an empire of the senses.

I've never been much of a one for deferred gratification – the only deferred gratification I'd ever be interested in would involve the shaving of someone's pubic hair, I tend to think – and because of this Butlin's could have been created especially for greedy, needy I-want-it-now little me. Forget the Nazi song 'Tomorrow Belongs To Me' – 'Butlin's Belongs To Me' was far more to the point.

By this time, my dad and I were starting to twig that perhaps, just *perhaps*, our socialist paradise might not be right around the corner. (Second star to the right and straight on till morning! Just clap your hands and Communism *will live*!) Life for our branch of the working class – upper, urban, king-making – was fast starting to resemble the last five minutes of *The Generation Game*, when the consumer goodies go by quick on a conveyor belt and what you name – fondue set, cuddly toy – you get. My father looked hard and long, and reported back to me with some relish that the working class were going at it 'like piggies at a trough'. All things being equal, we deserved to enjoy ourselves as the *Titanic* went down. For if Socialism is the bread of life, then Crazy Golf is the jam on it.

There was a Butlin's quite near us, at Minehead in Somerset, but my father, with characteristic thoroughness, valour and perversity, decided that the Butlin's boasted by Bognor Regis – at Sussex by the sea and on the other side of the country – was the thing. Seeing as how Butlin's camps were based on uniformity, this seemed as strange as insisting on visiting White City McDonald's when you live in Tower Hamlets. But I dare say he had his reasons – and the end result of our week-long annual revels spoke for themselves.

As I've said, my dad was a born leader of men. When men weren't available, preferably holding tools they could down copiously and quickly after one impromptu rabble-rouser from him, he was a born leader of dogs, women and children. Holidays brought this into play *in extremis*. I remain convinced that he alighted on Butlin's, Bognor Regis, simply because getting there involved more complicated machinations and manoeuvres than any other branch in the British Isles. Sure, there were camps in Skegness and beyond. But there were probably trains direct there from Bristol Temple Meads or something. One long train ride and a coach to meet you at the station at the most. And that would *never* have done.

Getting to Sussex, though, was lovely and difficult – an organizational nightmare and an organiser's dream date. My dad's leadership qualities were shown to their greatest advantage when all around him were losing their heads, so panic was the order of the day. On the morning of the trek the alarm clocks, which my father (claimed to have) wound the previous night, would fail to go off at five, finding my mother and me crying on the shivering summer landing at seven, while my dad instructed us to keep calm and rushed around packing, calling taxis and giving the dog a pep talk re. The Kennels.

Butlin's forbade dogs, so The Kennels were, reluctantly, the only option. Dogs – or rather, The Dog, as each of them was – holding the reflexively revered position they did in our household, we were taught to regard The Kennels as a last resort, like vasectomy, and never to be gone into lightly unless all other options had been exhausted. After an exceedingly traumatic *Stella Dallas* meets *Mildred Pierce* routine at The Kennels, my dad rising admirably to the part of the wronged hero sacrificing his own happiness (played by The Dog) for the benefit of others (my mother and me), there would be a mad rush for the train. We invariably left the house late, due to dog-related incidents and almost frenzied sandwich making, and I recall so many holidays which not ended but started in tears as my mother and I ran fearfully after my father through the underground tunnels of Bristol Temple Meads station.

Once on the train, though, we could settle down to the real point of the journey: changing trains. My father would sit there poring over the Bristol-to-Sussex timetables with the zeal of a fanatical gambler studying the day's form at Kempton, or a Red Guard the Little Red Book. No station was so small or out of the way that my dad couldn't manage to discover some essential change there. And, of course, our platform was *always* on the other side of the rickety wooden footbridge, up and down which my mother and I forever seemed to be running, weeping, after my ceaselessly striding father, our infernal trotting almost Looking-Glass worldish in its endless trajectory. But just when we were at our most weepy and footsore my father would step forward and point, like a piece of giant socialist-realist sculpture, towards the train bearing down on the Barnham platform. It was the one which, in the space of one stop and fifteen minutes, would transport us to another world: Butlin's, Bognor Regis.

I'll tell you one thing: the King wouldn't have said 'Bugger Bognor' on his deathbed if they'd had a Butlin's there then. He'd have risen from it, rolled up his trousers and entered the Knobbly Knees Contest. Sometimes, even now when I haven't been there for more than a quarter of a century, I still wonder what sort of monumentally miserabilist pip of a person could have looked upon Butlin's and its frenzied fiefdoms of fun and not had a good time. Like dour old Kenneth Tynan couldn't get an erection unless his paramour thought *Look Back In Anger* the greatest play ever written, I definitely couldn't get wet for anyone who couldn't have a complete and utter scream at Butlin's. It's no coincidence that in later years the camps would be used for forty-eight hour raves by the E Generation.

Arriving at the front office, which smugly overlooked Bognor's almost fiendishly dull sea front, you checked the Old You at the desk and went to find your chalet, where the limber, lithe, lissome and most definitely *not shy* New You awaited you, already having slipped into its sarong and sandals, smiling and sitting on the spartan single bed from where it rose, sand falling from its silky thighs, to shake your hand.

And then it was out, out, out – one always seemed to be stepping out through the door, into the sunlight and surrealism that was Butlin's at its best. And most wonderful of all, I could be *left alone* there. No doubt there was the odd child molester roaming those manicured lawns, a truly crazy golfer passing for normal in the first sitting for dinner at the very next table from my own happy family, looking at my legs where they wound out like expressways to delirium from my yellow corduroy hotpants and thinking unclean thoughts.

But there was no fear. And I was left, at last, triumphantly and conclusively alone to come and go as I pleased, as my parents whiled away their royally deserved holiday in the Pig and Whistle. My holidays at Butlin's, far from convincing me of the special role of the family in the life of a child, only went to reinforce what all those latchkey-kid years had: that if there was one thing I needed like a verruca on the vagina, it was *looking after*.

I lost something there, perhaps: my childhood, or any last remains of an idea that I needed protecting. A couple of years ago I read a letter, on a magazine problem page, from a girl with a strange affliction. Some years ago, she wrote, her parents had planned to take her on holiday which she had looked forward to with unparalleled excitement. They had gone on the holiday and she had loved it as much as she had thought she would. There was only one problem: she found herself day-dreaming of the lost holiday by day and nightmaring of it by night. She was convinced that *some important part of her* had *stayed* there when her body left; that she had enjoyed herself *so much* that she had, in a way, laughed herself to death.

In my dreams, I too chase something through the deserted camps; through the echoing swimming pools with the parrots hanging from the high glass ceilings, past the abandoned Crazy Golf courses and the deserted funfair where the merry-go-round broke down and the horses grin their wild-eyed rictus grin for ever with not even the strains of 'It's a Long Way To Tipperary' for solace, through the Beachcomber Lounge where the swimmers' legs move in eerie autonomy through the glass panels on the wall, around and around the outdoor pool where we finally catch the pirate and push him to his watery end. But everything's in the wrong place now and I can never find my way home.

Charlotte R just called and said she saw two possible titles for this book at the Natural History Museum. 'One was "Bright Eyed And Dangerous".'

'Ooo! I like that!'

'But the second one was better.'

'What was that then, my angel?'

'It was in the toilets. It was "Now Please Wash Your Hands".'

Some suggestions are simply beneath contempt.

CHAPTER THREE

I Died
Each Day

I think it was Kierkegaard who said that schooldays are the happiest days of our lives. If it wasn't him it was Jean-Paul Sartre or Nick Cave, or some other miserable basket whose one mission in life is to bring the party down and increase the suicide rate. By the way, my friend the crypto-Fascist academic – just kidding, Professor! – George Urban says that Hungary has the highest suicide rate in the world because of the Hungarian attitude to romantic love. Apparently it's not perfect and doesn't last for ever, or something along those lines. I personally think it's because of goulash.

At my comprehensive school we got goulash for lunch three times a week. There weren't any fancy alternative menus in those days either. Oh no! We weren't offered, as are today's kiddies, a lunch menu which looked something like this:

Truffles with foie gras and Guerande fleur de sel and chips
or
Linda McCartney's HomeStyle VegeBanger and chips
or
Freshly caught colinot, grilled on a wood fire, served with
lightly fried basil and chips
or

I Knew I Was Right

Sautéd head of clueless Sociology supply teacher and chips

Washed down with Evian, Vimto and an insouciant little
Chassagne-Montrachet '92

Two pounds twenty-five pence

We got goulash. And for one reason: *obviously none of us, working-class schoolchildren living in the England of the Nineteen Seventies, knew what goulash was meant to taste like.* Ha! So they could put what they liked in it. It was the Emperor's New Goulash; 'Oh, it's *meant* to taste like that. Haven't you ever visited the Austro-Hungarian Empire, then?' They couldn't give us paella because some of the posh girls had been to Torremolinos. No one had been to Hungary, not even Jayne Fyfoot who had a pony. Not even Elizabeth Powell in Form Two, who had moved here from – gasp! – Sidcup. She told everyone Sidcup was in London and was instantly invited into the In Crowd even though she looked like a troll. I was madly jealous of her, not because of the dumb old In Crowd, who had the debating skills of a bag of Dolly Mixtures, but because she came from *London*! I was childishly but justifiably pleased in adult life when I discovered that Sidcup was in Kent. Ha! Practically *Bristol*.

I was bitten early by the London lurgy. I became a *Capitalist*; not the people my dad swore at on the TV news, but someone who worshipped the capital city and invested it with all sorts of meanings and powers. From the age of ten, I kept a London Underground map on my wall, above my bed, watching over my silly, brilliant, sleeping head. I learned the stations by heart, the stations of the Cross: King's Cross, Angel, White City – to me they were the Promised Land, where at last I might truly Become Myself. I would stare at that map for hours, as if it would reveal the very mystery of life itself if only I stared long enough. I looked at it in the troubled, stricken, disorientated way that respectable men often look at women stripping. Don't let them ever tell you that art never changed anyone's life; Harry Beck, who designed the Tube map, changed and probably saved mine.

I wanted to go to London the way other people want to go to the bathroom: *because I have to or I'll burst!* I would work out what I was going to do there when I got there. Getting to London was, and is to this very day, the single most consuming desire I have ever known: more than any love, hate, or ambition. You've heard of that saying 'You can't get there from here'? Well, I couldn't get to any sort of life worthy of the name from Bristol: I knew as surely as I knew my own name that if I stayed I would get fucked, pregnant, married. And after that I wouldn't get anything but old.

I think of my youth – that is, the time between ten and seventeen, when I exchanged the hard currency of my *newness* for a career of evil (Dr Faustus, I presume!) and became a sort of Teenage Impersonator, Danny La Rue in Lewis Leathers – as a long, sad series of waiting-rooms, one opening onto the other, like an Escher impression of a dentist's. Boy, did I wait! – in my pram, teething, my First Little Weapons pushing painfully through my smooth, secret gums; in my playpen, ripping up my books because *they just weren't good enough* (ever the critic); in Double Maths, wanting to die, literally, because I couldn't see the board and I couldn't see the point, decimal or otherwise; in dance halls, dreading the slow tunes, hiding in the toilets, wanting to weep at the sight of my adored Nicola Latham in the arms of some recently escaped Bristol Zoo ape; in my long summer holidays blind with reading, snowblind with non-specific needing.

But most of all, I waited in My Room; waited to Be Somebody. Then and only then would I truly be Myself; then I could cast off this ignoble incognito and reclaim my life. I was like the hero at the end of *A Tale Of Two Cities*, going to the gallows because they thought he was someone else. Well, they obviously thought I was, too – someone who worked in factories, said 'Pardon' and let men who'd never even read *A Rebours* in *translation* maul her about! Well, *we'll see.*

I don't remember ever feeling like a child, despite my parents' exemplary provision of protection, security and love. I think some of it was to do with being an only child – weird people at the best of times. In the summer of 1996 Laura Lockington and I founded three clubs, all of which we are the sole members of: the How Dare You Club (too arcane to explain), the Indestructible Ten Per Cent Club (self-explanatory) and the Only Child Club. The last one is the most important and the most fiercely coveted. One girl even asked me seriously if she would be eligible for membership if her brother died. 'Accidentally,' she added quickly.

Being an only child is vital to me; it is, as our American friends say, *part of who I am*, and I still feel a pang of illogical disappointment on hearing that someone I have grown fond of is not an only child. We are outnumbered in a houseful of adults; we go undercover, make ourselves clever, in order to join and then beat them. If you have a sibling you always have a safety net. Only children are orphans who have parents; the best of both worlds, when it comes to growing up fast and smart. ('And sociopathic,' says Charlotte Raven helpfully. 'Don't forget that one!' Cheers, Charlotte.)

Reading was another reason I put aside childish things before I lost my milk teeth. Reading – it's the weirdest thing in the world. It looks like the most passive activity known to man; people who give 'reading' as their hobby qualify themselves as automatic wall-flowers. Yet reading has rocked more worlds, turned more heads, changed more lives than sex, drugs and Nintendo put together. The word 'escapism', used of leisure pursuits, is nowadays a bad one, conjuring up pap, placebos and palliatives, the James Bond, the Mills and Boon. But books, even pulp ones, can literally help you *escape* the shallow grave of your alleged life. Because you see another world, and seeing is believing, and believing becomes *leaving*.

It kills me when middle-class kids see Not Reading as some sort of rebellion. If you don't read books, you really have been fucked over in a major way. You have been castrated and conned. To read, voluntarily, is the first step to asserting the fact that *you know that there is somewhere else*. This is a criticism of where you are, of course. And a terrible insult to the people who know they'll never Get Out Of Jail Free. On my first day at comprehensive school I was mocked, pilloried and finally punched for reading in the playground. They thought I was being snooty – it was a *James Bond book*, for the love of Mike: *Live And Let Die*! I was already well into Graham Greene, but I'd chosen it on purpose so as not to make the wretched oiks feel bad about themselves. And that's the thanks I get.

Comprehensive school. The Big Playground. I really couldn't get my head around it and that's where the trouble – and my life as I know it today – started. Not feeling like a child had, for some reason, worked OK at the Infants and Juniors – probably because they were infantile and juvenile, and didn't have the radar to pick up the stark staring fact that I was a pretend Mixed Infant, fresh as the moment when my Pod went pop! At Big School, while by no means intellectual – or even sentient, if we're being brutally frank – the kids are big enough to have been thoroughly trained by their parents and teachers; trained to be conformist, tiny-minded and totally mistrustful of the outside world. Looking back, this is, spiritually at least, where Thatcherism came from; from clever working- and lower-middle-class children who were bullied simply for being bright by their clod-hopping contemporaries. Scratch a Thatcherite and find an outsider; Morrissey with mone-tarism instead of miserabilism. And it leaves one with very little fellow feeling or loyalty to the lower classes, believe you me. I had to work like a black – or rather a Bengali – to get mine back.

My school uniform was as follows: navy-blue skirt, yellow shirt, brick-red jumper, red, yellow and blue tie, a snood sprinkled with stardust and nipple clamps. (I lied about the last two.) In summer, blue check dress with navy-blue cardigan. Blue. Yellow. Red. You don't need it at that age, do you? You want to paint it black, not stride about like the Stars and Stripes gone mad. I have a Handy Pre-Millennial Hint here for schools who have trouble making their troublesome teenage pupils wear the correct uniform. Make it black. Pure, sheer, unrelieved black – the only hint of colour being a gash of scarlet on the mouth. (Especially for the lads.) Within weeks you'll see results.

What is most important to realise about your teenage years is *how bad the In Crowd feel about themselves*. It's not much consolation when they're shoving your head down a toilet pan and pulling the chain – but *they really do feel empty* behind all that swank and swagger. An American book called *Is There Life After High School?*, published in the Seventies, painted a convincing picture of the Queen and King of the Prom heading straight for a mobile home in Montana and a job as a meat-packer; the outsiders, on the other hand, found that the only way was up. When we think of the sad adolescent memories of all the great film beauties from Marilyn Monroe to Kim Basinger to Uma Thurman, we hear the same thing over and over; that they were wallflowers at best, pariahs at worst. The King and Queen of the Prom just *know*, in their heart of hearts, that their lives will effectively end the day they walk through those school gates for the last time. And they know that the oddballs will thrive in the world outside. That's why they stick your head down the toilets. Bless.

Not that *they* were holding *my* head down it – the In Crowd. When I started at Brislington Comprehensive school – 'Bris', as it was known in the local argot, an uninspired boxy little building situated stupidly near to St Brendan's, a stuck-up Roman Catholic public school whose pupils we called 'Brendas' and whom we ritually, girls and boys both, beat up on the last day of term – the In Crowd were an awesome bunch of Suedehead girls with feather cuts, crombies and two-tone brogues, who struck fear into the heart of us freshmen by staggering around the dank corridors of the school in break- and lunch-time holding each other up and yelling repeatedly, to the tune of 'Day-Oh', 'Nuts! Whole Hazelnuts – oooph! Cadbury's take them and they cover them with choc-o-late!' This chant, strangely, a harmless hymn to a popular confection and already very familiar from the Cadbury's Whole-Nut television commercial, had an air of dark tribal menace which, for me at least, has never been exceeded by any other piece of music. When I saw the film *If...*, while the famous African chant, the 'Missa Luba Sanctus' motif, held a *germ* of the primitive might and mystery of 'Nuts! Whole Hazelnuts – Oooph', it evoked mere unease, whereas its blueprint brought forth unadulterated fear and trembling.

It is an old, tired lie that what the United States of America does at any given time, Britain will do soon afterwards. It is, since the rock'n'roll explosion of the 1950s, almost impossible to find any new thing about which America has hula-hooped itself into the usual state of hysteria which Britain has leapt upon with any degree of eagerness. It might be indeed – though also unlikely – statistically closer to the truth to say that 'What Sweden does today, Britain will do next year' or even 'What Mongolia does today, Blighty will do tomorrow teatime.'

School is one such case in point. Think about the institution of the American High School. It is an inky-fingered fiefdom, a hickey-covered hierarchy in which roles are cast in iron and set in steel. Whether you are from the right or the wrong side of the tracks, whether you are a virgin or a slut, whether you are pretty or plain – that is all that matters. It is often wrongly stated that American society is highly individualistic. This is a lie. What it is is *selfish*, not at all the same thing. Lacking as it does any firm, organic social structure, America grabs frantically at conformity as its security blanket. This explains the widespread American phenomenon of the business 'convention' at which to be truly conventional, a precise clone of the next guy, is the apex of all earthly ambition.

Similarly, the American High School practises a kind of teeny-bopper apartheid; in films like *The Breakfast Club*, we saw how it was perfectly possible for students in the same year, the same form, to pass through their secondary educations without once talking to a classmate from a different group; the greasers, jocks, swots, nerds, hippies. It's not the same here.

Here, or at least in the foreign country which was a Bristol comprehensive school in the 1970s, what mattered was whether or not you were 'hard'. If you were, you could be drop-dead smart like Bambi Bamford or fall-down dumb like Susan Jones. You could be a loud-mouthed yobette like Carol Longden or a softly spoken Zen-calm breeze like Elizabeth 'Lil' Hudd – who was also, it should be noted here, the most sexually admired and desired girl in my year, right from Mixed Infants. Lil had short brown hair, milk-bottle glasses and a straight-up-and-down figure; she came from a poor but honest family and wore the same dress day in, day out. But I rather think that she must have been the first girl I met who had 'It'; hard nuts turned to soft runny centres, even pastel girly fondant cremes, at the mention of her name. She was also amazingly nice and seemed not to notice her popularity. Hard, though, she undoubtedly was.

Somehow, I found myself at the age of twelve – just one year after entering the comprehensive system, an absolute aesthete and literary snob to boot, already hip to Nabokov and Graham Greene – hanging with the Hard Girls. I had fully expected to be an outsider, but something happened: as random and inevitable as my dark blonde hair catching the sun ('She's got *natural streaks*,' I heard one Hard Girl hissing at another as I walked by one summer's day) or my aggravating personality catching a detention. Detentions are what English Hard Girls have instead of sororities: you went there not to be punished by teachers, but to be viewed and evaluated by the In Crowd. From the moment I walked in and sat down I could feel Carol Longden and Rosalyn Lapthorne, the hardest girls in my year, whispering about me:

'She's got a Ben Sherman! Sue Jones saw her downtown.'

'Yeah, well? She's always *reading*. She *reads* on the *bus*.'

'Look, she'll probably *stop* when she's got proper mates.'

'She's been *offered* proper mates, Ros! Bambi Bamford's *always* liked her! She don't care! She'd rather *read a book* than go downtown! 'Sides, she don't have a Saturday job . . .'

I tried to concentrate on my lines. But it was dead difficult, being so close to the path of true glory. As we left the detention class I saw Rosalyn and Carol muttering in the cloakroom and I knew they were talking about me. I bowed my head in deference and made as if to walk on by.

'Oi! You!' said Carol rudely.

I looked up. 'Me?'

'Over 'ere!'

I went towards them. Rosalyn, a dainty little doll of a girl, stepped smartly aside as Carol, a beautiful bruiser, caught me

smartly by the school tie and swung me up against the coat pegs. It
hurt. 'Oww!'

'Shut it!' Carol instructed urgently. You'd have thought I was
on the verge of joining the SAS. She Who Dares Feather Cuts.
'Look! You want to go about, or what?'

Well, there was surely only one answer. But over Carol's shoulder, Rosalyn mouthed 'yes', just in case I hadn't tumbled yet.

'Yeah, 'course.' I sneered at Carol, truly believing that dumb
insolence would surely seal the deal like nothing else.

'Good.' She punched me casually and chronically in the
stomach. 'And don't ever look at me like that again.'

So now I was officially 'hard'. And the first thing I had to take
on board was that behaviour such as Carol's was *in no way* violent;
it was simply the Hard Girl equivalent of shaking hands. For hardness, among teenage girls of the time, had nothing to do with violence but, I suppose, with 'keeping yourself tidy' to a quite
pathological degree. It was about doing all the stuff that *should*
have made you a mess – and somehow remaining completely unaf-
fected by it. In a way, it was a blow-dried lip-glossed continuation
of the High Noon gun-fighter myth.

In practice, this code of platform-heeled honour meant that you
had to drink an ocean of Pernod and Black at the Sugared Almond
on a Saturday night – but you never stumbled, you never wept and
you never once even indicated your inclination to indulge in a
yawn of the Technicolor variety. That signified you as a social
leper, which was not hard. You had to have every desirable boy in
the entire school (all two of them, heh heh) dying to 'go out' with
you (a misnomer, as 'going out' in this case invariably meant 'staying in', as likely as not baby-sitting for your young married neighbours, probably called Lynn and Martin, the baby to be known as
Samantha to civilians, 'Sammy' to the family, because if you went
out both his friends and your friends would see the pair of you and
it just wouldn't look hard, basically) but you certainly didn't sleep
with anyone. That signified you as a slag, which was not hard. You
had to be seen to put no effort whatsoever into your schoolwork,
but you certainly didn't show anything as sloppy as rebellion in

any way – rebellion was ''ippie' and, worse than 'ippie, rebellion was 'squatter' – the worst possible word of abuse in my set. Squatters, perversely, represented all that was not 'ard, proud, sound to us heartless teenymonsters; squatters showed, God forbid, *emotion*. Looking back, I see that a lot of the distinguishing characteristics of being 'ard in we selected adolescents were the same as the signifiers of autism in a child. We mistook cold for cool; to be frank, we mistook a dirty great Arctic wasteland of the soul for an Arctic Roll. It just *felt* so good; I sneer, therefore I am.

Violence, following on from this frostbitten code of honour, was also seen as not 'ard; the female physical role models of our group were, sickeningly, Olivia Newton-John with her doe eyes and perfect centre parting and the prancing poltroons of Pan's People, particularly Cherry, the winsome dark piece.

I hated Pan's People with every new pence of my passion; lividly young, thin and beautiful at twelve, I felt no physical envy whatsoever (don't forget, my generation grew up under the skinny, sallow shadow of June Bolan; we were quite sceptical about the power of looks, especially having watched Yoko Ono and Linda McCartney wreck the universes of our older sisters before us) but rather a real class war hatred of them. At this point, I must point out, I was emerging from a tempestuous, soul-destroying seven-year on-off relationship with ballet, at which I had shown real promise, but for which I had grown (a) too tall and (b) too hard. What my height started my friends finished off, and in the end I sneeringly renounced it and gave my beautiful satin *pointe* shoes to the tot next door for her dressing-up box. But for at least two years after I gave up ballet there were few Tuesday nights – the night of my lesson – when I didn't cry myself to sleep, remembering those years from five to twelve when reading on one hand and ballet on the other provided me with twin escape hatches of slippery bliss down which to slide free of the heart-breaking banality of my alleged 'life'.

Typically, my father, while loathing any form of effeminacy in men to the point where he had to leave the room, should either Lionel Blair or Gene Kelly appear suddenly on the television, to prevent himself from becoming wildly and uncharacteristically violent, took me religiously – literally religiously, with a face on him like a really butch old martyr going stolidly on his way to the stake – to the Bristol Hippodrome twice a year to view whatever ballet companies were passing through; I saw the Ballet Rambert, the Royal Ballet and the Bolshoi, plus a whole lot more not so leading lights. I don't believe, though, that I ever saw the Elmhurst Ballet Company – Elmhurst being the ballet school where every wussy little middle-class slag went whose only acquaintance with rhythm came when she was trying to work out which days of the month she wouldn't get pregnant from shagging the gardener, rolling around like a two-backed swine in the filthy dripping compost of her class's moribund slime, the bitch!

Gosh! I'm *sorry* about that. But I guess you sort of understand me by now, after eighteen thousand words, every one of them a *cry for help* (because it is so difficult to get good servants these days, after all) and you sort of know that it was, like, really *hard* for me, carrying about this great big jagged glittering brain in my little noodle, a brain as fragmented and beautiful and shimmering as the nests those lovely Bower Birds of David Attenborough's make for themselves, when I was ceaselessly aware, the blood thumping like a boxer with a medicine ball day and night in the same singular little noodle, that I was promised to the conveyor belt and the multiple pregnancy sired by an escaped ape at the age of sweet sixteen. Ah. Bless. So it made me a bit *twisted*, see. Not only did middle-class girls have a *life* as their birthright; they had ballet. One could be an accident; two is what I think they call the filthy, unfair, septic English class system.

So I *hated* Pan's People. They had all been to *ballet school*, apparently, had they? I would snarl at the wisest and most trustworthy of my friends. Really? Well, a bigger bunch of flat-footed clodhoppers it would have been hard to find this side of the Bristol Zoo Elephant House, in my humble thirteen-year-old opinion. Interestingly, their 'talent', if it could by any stretch of the imagination be called that, decreased in proportion to their sex appeal; big blonde Babs, undoubtedly the loveliest of the lot, looked as though she was literally being *thrown* back on to the stage by some invisible giant's hand whenever she returned to terra firma from any given jeté. Dee Dee, a prim, thin-lipped filly, on the other hand, could just about get her head around an arabesque without falling flat on her face.

'Excuse me? Pan? Wasn't he, like, *a good dancer*?' I would moan ritually each Friday morning to my all-seeing, non-judging friend Bambi Bamford. 'Couldn't they have been called Morpheus's Minions? Because, like, they seem to be sleep-walking or something?'

'You've got to get over this Pan's People thing, Jul,' Bambi would advise, spitting on to her block of Miners mascara and peering happily, as well she might, into the incorporated mirror. Bambi looked like a heroine from a Jackie story strip, all huge melting eyes, long legs, miniskirt, maxicoat and, as it turned out, eternal youth. She died in a car crash in her seventeenth summer. She shone.

The best Big Hate and Loathing moments came tinged with derision and pity during those odd weeks when Pan's People were forced to dance to novelty records, either with animals – 'Get Down' by Gilbert O'Sullivan, when dogs kept trying to shag their legs (talk about type-casting) – or pretending to be them – 'Funky Gibbon' by The Goodies when you *really were forced to wonder* whether God gave Man free will after all.

'*Really*, Jul,' said Bambi, stroking sticky plum shader beneath her Mount Rushmore cheekbones. 'I *mean*.'

I watched *Top Of The Pops* without fail, the way I listened to the new Radio One chart every Tuesday lunch-time at school with my ear pressed up against a sad transistor, as we all did in those days; grimly, with an ever-present edge of potential hysteria. For teenage girls in the early Seventies, listening for the new chart each Tuesday lunchtime was the nearest we would ever get to the feeling our grandparents had had when they listened to Chamberlain's speech declaring war on Germany. Ashen faces were everywhere and Lesley Ellett's breathy little voice would invariably be raised in pain as Alice Cooper slid three places to number 69. Things were often pretty damn grim in that bunker we laughably called a cloakroom, let me tell you. When such living monstrosities as 'Grandad' by Clive Dunn or 'Ernie' by Benny Hill put down roots in the top slot for months on end, I sometimes feared a mass suicide *à la* Jamestown, substituting Tizer for Kool-Aid. And I say without fear that I believe I can trace several instances of later mental illness in the young women of Bristol right back to the living hell that was one nation under the iron thumb of 'Eye Level' (theme from *Van Der Valk*) by the Simon Park Orchestra.

But in those days the Chart was the Chart and to gripe at it seemed as futile as arguing with God. Music *is* tremendously precious to most teenagers; I seriously believe that it has saved more young lives than the Samaritans and my writing put together. And so I've been thinking about how actually to deal with music in this mischievous little memoir of mine. The recent recollections of the Seventies Experience have given *massive* importance to music – but, blush, they were of course written by *boyzzz*. The sort of boy, it must be said, who grew up to be a man who'd see leaving the inner sleeve off a Richard and Linda Thompson record as quite reasonable grounds for divorce (mental cruelty). The kind who'd take out two weeks a year to re-label his cassettes and if he ran out of ink while he was doing it would not dream of continuing the job until he found *exactly the shade* of ink and *exactly the size* of nib. A right little party animal, in fact. As in Lib-Dems. Personally, the only thing I want to retain anally is my boyfriend during sex.

See? It's different for girls. By and large, girls get to love pop music because it provides such a glorious soundtrack to their shiny new lives. Without meaning to be rude, the sort of boys who get obsessed, *really* obsessed with pop music do so because they don't have a life. We did, in our own small way, full of psychodramas and crushes and clothes crises. To us, pop music was an Overture and Beginners, there to warm us up for the evening ahead. Or it was a way to be allowed to *scream*, to show the emotions of frustration, anger and exhilaration which girls are trained out of so brutally and unfairly from the moment they can squawk, let alone walk or talk.

Because the world is basically about men murdering women, you see, in one form or another, be it metaphorically through marriage or mutilatory through massacre, men *know* that women have every right to be *really angry*. And that if we ever did wake up and smell the bride's blood, we'd run amok and kill the lot of them. 'If one woman told the truth, the world would crack apart,' a famous Russian lady poet once said. And so our anger is locked up, isolated in the West Wing with Mr Rochester's allegedly 'mad' wife. And it comes out in harmless, charming little ways like self-mutilation, bulimia and anorexia instead of the way it should come out, which is in a fair number of male deaths. Women, bless 'em! – inside, we're all shoveable.

But we *are* allowed to scream at teen stars – 'scream stars', I was the first pop writer ever to call them. And a good thing, because the scream star really is the truest, the most honest, the most useful type of crooner, really *used* and then put aside like the perfect out-played pop single. By the time you're seventeen, your one and only life should not be revolving around a rotating piece of plastic; that's just living your life in a playpen, with you as the baby and the dummy both. Girls have pop, which sees them through; boys have rock, which keeps them in.

So I was ready, willing and able to be hard. I had the shirt – Ben Sherman – the single – 'Band of Gold' – and the peer group. But I was always just passing for normal. When the bullying started, finally, from my group, it was very minor. But I saw red. My eyes blind with blood, I pushed out my hands like paws.

'Steady!' Bambi reminded me. 'Leave it, Jul! Just let it alone! It's over!'

But it wasn't. ''Ere . . . Onion 'Ead,' the leader of the gang taunted a dreadfully ugly girl whose head did indeed seem to sprout at its summit very much in the manner of said vegetable. 'Why's your 'ead like a . . . onion?'

We looked at the alleged root as one; the good, the bad, the ugly, but all of us the Hard Girls. Hard as nails; the nails in the coffin of our compassion, our chance for future empathy, for a free ride into the empire of imagination.

'Well, *why?*'

I drew a deep breath.

'*Julie,*' Bambi said in my ear, and it was her own name, our name, a name full of both the sweetness and hardness of working-class girl-children. '*Julie . . .*'

'Ohhh!' I exclaimed, cannoning into Onion Head and standing where she had stood until then. She toppled into the dust, but that wasn't the *point.* 'Ohhh, no! I really don't *think* so! No!'

Sue and George got a good thumping in before Bambi ushered the Hard Girls away, shooting me daggers with her hot-toddy eyes. *It's not clever and it's not cool,* her flint face said to me before turning away, leaving me to face my fate; the first Hard Girl ever to cross the floor and side with the nerds. *Death.*

I turned to look at them, feeling pretty good. They weren't cute like my gang, but Hell. 'So!' I said brightly. 'How's tricks?'

Onion Head's nasty synthetic satchel caught me square on the vulnerable back of the neck; Ruth the spastic kicked me with both relish and rhythm as I sprawled there on the merciless macadam of the big playground. As the freaks gathered and my body became a pulsating mass of pain (only without the good bits you get with sex) I saw what Bambi had been trying to say to me. How she suffered for her sanity . . . *We had made these people outcasts for a very good reason – because they were weird and nasty as all fuck! And now, through my own wanton and random outbreaks of compassion, I was one of them!*

How very, *very* appropriate.

Charlotte just called. 'Call your book "Confidential Destruction".' She saw it on the side of a lorry. I think not.

CHAPTER FOUR

Career
of Evil

In 1975 unemployment was to hit one million British souls for the first time. Me, I already had my work cut out.

I certainly had a long furrow to hoe if I was going to make it yet as Most Popular Girl in the School, or even at any given time in the toilets, and that was for sure. But only slightly ahead of me now, coming closer every waking hour, chasing me like the Fugitive after the one-armed man, was something even more depressing than the protracted silences and preternatural sneers of the schoolyard.

'Educate' may well mean 'I lead out' in Latin; in working-class Bristolian it means 'I lock in. And throw away the key.' There may indeed be a tradition in such exotic kingdoms as Wales and Scotland for *encouraging* one's children and *wanting* them to do better than you did, but I'm damned if it ever made it as far east or south as poor little me. I ignored it as long as I could, I gambolled in the Indian summer sunshine like a trouper – but the long tall shadow of the gallows always hung over my childish play and my busy blackberrying and my piously point-scoring contributions to the Harvest Festivals.

And then there was the shadow of The Factory.

You know that old rhyme, 'Tinker, Tailor, Soldier, Sailor – Rich Man, Poor Man, Beggarman, Thief'? In Bristol, in the

Nineteen Seventies, ours went 'Factory worker, office worker, factory worker, office worker – factory worker, office worker, gymslip mother, thief's girlfriend'. I'm not joking. My social and career horizons, when I was growing up, made the average pit pony look like Yuri Gagarin. No, I tell a lie ('Often!' – C. Raven) – that should probably be 'Factory worker, office worker, factory worker, teacher training college'. I'm not kidding; if you lived round our way and your intelligence went way, way off the scale, you might conceivably be offered a place at teacher training college. If Einstein had been growing up in Bristol in the Seventies he'd have ended up at teacher training college in Cardiff, fiddling with his Bics like a mad thing and asking bilious girls from Bangor back to his digs for Bournvita.

Well, if there was one thing I didn't need it was to spend the rest of my life trying to grind any dates into the Hard Girls other than the ones they were going on tonight with Lee Williams or Richard Chaffey down Raquel's Discotheque. I wasn't considered *clever* enough to go to teacher training college, anyway. Ha! So I found myself gazing squarely and unfairly at the typing pool and the factory floor.

You know that Bruce Springsteen song 'Factory'? 'Through the mansions of fear / Through the mansions of pain / See my daddy walking through those factory gates in the rain / Factory takes his hearing / Factory gives him life / The work, the working, just the working life.' I didn't know it when I was twelve, because it hadn't been written then, but I went one better; I saw the live show, one performance only, never to be repeated or forgotten.

In the media, though it's meant to be a whole big wide world of *arrivistes* and counter-jumpers, very few people can really get their heads around what it feels like to be the daughter of two first-generation-literate factory hands who ends up hearing Elizabeth Archer of *The Archers* and Karen Grant of *Brookside* both claiming within the space of six months that their ambition is to be 'the next Julie Burchill'. Julie who? Who, me?

'You were an answer today,' my mother told me on the phone a while ago.

'I was a what?' Good Lord, had the woman finally seen the light at long last?

'An *answer*. On a *quiz*. On the telly. I had to sit down. It felt all funny.'

Well, *yes*. All funny but really, really pleasant, if the truth be told, to be one of the tiny tribe of working-class girl-children who had grown up to bestride a profession whose idea of an *arriviste* counter-jumper was until then Tina Brown, of Knightsbridge and Oxbridge – my dear, her father was a *film producer!*

I am gladder than words can wield the matter that I have become successful as a writer. My life, I believe, has been as gorgeous as anyone's could possibly get. I never, ever wish I had clung to my roots – roots are for trees, not people, and even on trees they often warp and tangle and have to be cut away in the interests of the higher survival. And I never wish I'd been born middle class, because then I'd have to hate myself for being a pisspoor prannet and that would be self-loathing and self-loathing's unhealthy, innit? Obviously I haven't been harmed in any way visible to the naked eye (heh heh heh).

But nevertheless, living through my adolescence at the time was far, far worse than the idea of a lousy adolescence my middle-class media-tosser friends believe they had. Because on top of the fact that my skin made the Rocky Mountains look like chiffon velvet, my hormones were doing a mazurka and I could barely lift a pen with the burden of masturbation that fell heavily upon me each nightshift. (Where's everyone else? Bloody slackers! OK, I guess I'll have to *do it all myself.*) I was faced with parents who basically told me, whenever I got up the guts to raise a peep of hope for my brilliant future, that I was destined for life as a zombie. There was simply no arguing about it. As kind and compassionate a pair as you could hope to meet in every other area of life, when it came to my future my parents were vandals, Thought Police, judge and jury combined. And the verdict came in, loud and clear, eight days a week; that Miss Nobody from Nowhere was definitely not up for a visa or even an Awayday.

I think they didn't want me to have my feelings hurt. They

thought that if I tried to leave my earthbound milieu, I might do an Icarus and injure myself fatally. I *hope* that's the reason. We don't talk about it. We don't need to now, anyway. Which is probably the best of all possible worlds.

So I realised very early on that when it came to my brilliant career, I could rely on no one but myself. I was, effectively, alone in the world, because I wanted to be in the *big* world and my parents refused to acknowledge either it or my possible place in it. So I was, spiritually and intellectually, an orphan with only her own cool little head and her hot little hands to trust in. I did two things: I learned to write and I learned to shoplift. I saw them both as planning and practising for the future . . . and as revenge.

I don't know why some people have the urge to make up stories and some don't, but I'd bet it's got something to do with, when you're still a child, realising you've been given the wrong life. By writing, by trying all those different doors, you never know – you might just *stumble on your real one*! 'Aha – you are my Life and I claim my compensation!'

Another reason has got to be a certain collision of putative hedonism and potential intelligence when young. If you're meant to be a writer, you enjoy it; not in a wholesome, gung-ho, tone-deaf, ten-thousand-words-a-day Jeffrey Archer kind of way, but in a way that makes you feel nervous and nauseous before, and sleek and secret afterwards – like having really excellent sex with someone you're not meant to be having it with. That's why doing good writing is a bastard, in both senses: it's dead hard to do, but it's also a love child.

By the age of twelve I found myself lodged well into the crotch of the first of many paradoxes. I was – cue the Wall of Sound – a Rebel, but also one hundred per cent a girrrl; I was thrill-seeking to the extreme, but contrarily a complete physical coward. Therefore I had to find some occupation for my idle hands which might also lead to future accomplishment and eventual escape. I saw accomplishment as the rope ladder that snakes down from the rescuing helicopter in the final frame of action flicks, whisking me away from the burning-with-boredom building of my life, by then utterly gutted in more ways than one. I'd already discovered self-abuse; now it was time for self-advancement.

One Christmas I persuaded my parents to buy me an ancient manual typewriter. It was so old and so heavy that my father had to move it from room to room for me and even a big strong man like him was inevitably bent over its weight. When I think of someone whose words drop as heavy as stones, graceless, lumpen and clumping – my first husband, say – I always visualise Baby's First Typewriter. How suitable it would have been for him, bless him!

When I was safely ensconced in my bedroom, banging away through prime time and beyond at all sorts of juvenilia (mostly to do with sex and drugs, neither of which I'd ever come within sniffing distance of, or if I had my nose must have been very blocked up that day), my parents would take it in turns to desert their quiz shows and shit-coms in order to peep around the door and check that I wasn't up to no good. (As if!) 'Doing nice typing?' they'd enquire. *Typing*. It's a wilful misunderstanding, isn't it? This reminds me of what my homegirl Suzanne Moore's mum used to say when *her* working-class daughter showed signs of growing up shiny: 'Suzanne's reading. She's a bit depressed.'

So I'd nod furiously, bent pressed with my nose practically touching the keys due to violent short sight, and my middle finger of the right hand – the only finger I've ever been able to type with and which Tom Shone once called Demon Finger, and another time the whole hand Thing, after the talented hand in *The Addams Family* – travelling at a hundred miles an hour across the looming metal heights of my beautiful machine, and I'd run my inky finger through my sweaty hairline and mumble frantically to myself.

'Good,' they'd say bovinely and trundle back to Bob Monkhouse.

Sometimes I wished it had been the nuthouse instead. There were times when I must admit it crossed my mind that my parents might literally be insane. Couldn't they *see* what was in front of them? Did they really think that any teenage girl, however dim, got into this sort of state over her w.p.m.? God! It made me want to *puke* to think that all over the country there were millions of middle-class parents literally worshipping the ground their mediocre little Tims and Imogens walked on and telling them, in no uncertain terms, that *tomorrow belonged to them*. And what belonged to me? A typewriter I couldn't lift and a one-way ticket to Nowhere-on-Sea. Cheers!

Sometimes I used to look at glossy society magazines. I particularly . . . 'liked' is not the word, but I was fascinated in a morbid way by *Harpers & Queen*. I liked to read about the society girls chronicled in 'Jennifer's Diary' and as a writer I particularly enjoyed their names; apart from Communism, perfume and sex, girls' names have always been my favourite thing and it was inevitable – come the hour, come the houri – that if you stuck someone called *Charlotte Raven* in front of me, I'd have fallen incandescently in love with her even if she'd looked like a three-day-old omelette.

The ones who always stuck in my mind were Tara Money-Tooth and Nicola Wyldbore-Smith. Tara T-M was obviously just a joke, but the name and unknown ghost of Nicola Wyldbore-Smith stayed with me throughout my adolescence. I thought she sounded beautiful and I damned her. With every Spam sandwich I ate, every polyester party dress I donned, every factory job I balked at the thought of, the spectre of the gorgeously named Nicola Wyldbore-Smith floated in front of me. I hated her and I wanted her to die so that she could be reincarnated as me and just *see* how the other half live; how the youth of the other half are never allowed to live.

Interruption for spooky bit! Cue Twilight Zone *music – nee-na-nee-na-nee-na!*

One golden morning in the summer of 1996 in Brighton, the town with which I am as besotted as one only usually is with a lover (Brighton is the first place I ever *chose* to live; Bristol I was born in and London I had to get a life in, but this one is all about soul), I lay with the newspapers by the sea front arcade where my wonderful ten-year-old son played the machines. I tingled from the thrill

63

of starting the day by opening an envelope to find a dirty great cheque from a publisher and the anticipation of ending the day in the arms of the one I love, hurtling down that velvet-lined tunnel towards the bright white light of a singular new level of orgasm. After fifteen years in the twin institutions for the insane we call marriage and London, I felt squeaky clean, washed new with freedom. I felt that I had truly become myself at last.

I opened the *Daily Mail* and I read the following:

Squalid Death of Girl from the County Set

She seemed to have everything. Her family home was a 14th century estate, she rode with the Belvoir Hunt. Her father was a friend of Lady Thatcher.

But Nicola Wyldbore-Smith was found dying on a pavement of a rundown council estate after falling from a fifth-floor window of a shabby block of flats, an inquest heard yesterday.

The youngest daughter of Major-General Sir Brian Wyldbore-Smith CB, DSO, OBE was addicted to heroin, drinking a bottle of whisky a day and using crack cocaine, Westminster coroner Sir Anthony Barton was told.

She was said to be depressed because a close friend with whom she wanted to have a relationship was returning to his native Portugal. The 43-year-old was alone in his flat in North Kensington when she fell.

Dr Barton recorded an open verdict after hearing that she had suffered from mental problems in addition to her addiction, and that there was no suicide note and no evidence that she intended to kill herself.

Afterwards Sir Brian – the former director of the Conservative Party's Board of Finance, who was knighted in 1980 and whose Army career included acting as an assistant to Field Marshal Montgomery – refused to comment.

Miss Wyldbore-Smith's younger brother, Eton-educated Robin, 34, said her death was an accident caused by the type of window. 'There is no question of her having taken her own life,' he said.

'She was a very sweet, kind, gentle person – a most lovable person. The drug problem was all in the past. She had beaten it.'

Yesterday those who knew Miss Wyldbore-Smith spoke of the troubled privately educated girl who grew up to be an unhappy woman.

'She started off by trying to live her life the way her parents wanted her to, going hunting and all that, but she never really fitted into that scene,' recalled a friend from her youth in Grantham, Lincolnshire. 'She wasn't at all Right-wing, she was more into green politics, and was into a hippy life-style.'

Her decision to leave her hometown, where she ran a craft shop called Tumbleweed, for London brought her into a world for which she was ill-equipped to cope.

She bought a three-bedroom flat in affluent Maida Vale and the shy girl who wanted to make some friends began hanging around the trendy bars of Portobello Road.

A neighbour, Leslie Baillie, said: 'She had a hard life because of drugs, even though she came from a good family. Despite all her money, it didn't seem to make her happy.'

I looked at the photograph of Nicola Wyldbore-Smith in 1973, when I'd first seen her name and wished to see her dead, and I was shocked to see what a plain, ordinary woman she had been. Far from the spun-sugar silver-spooned supersonic golden girl I had conjured up as a demonic, vengeful thirteen-year-old, my eternal etherised enemy, she had been a misfit, lumpy as an old mattress in body and soul. Leaving her home town for London, fear in her stomach, not covered, 'into a world for which she was ill-equipped to cope . . .'

Stop me if you've heard this one.

Just like *me*, I marvelled, lying there shameless and blameless in the Brighton sun. Yet I had survived and thrived. While she . . .

Yesss! Inside the rough, nasty, untamed terrain of my brain, a fierce little cheerleader for the team called the working class, charred and merciless, began to wave her pompoms to a jungle beat, dancing fiercely like Josephine Baker transported from the

Folie Bergères to the front line of the class war. But the part of me that was free turned away and wept.

I moved my tears through briskly, like a tour guide processing visitors to a stately home. Neither glee nor sorrow was the correct response to the death of Nicola Wyldbore-Smith. Only a vast, weary acceptance of the vagaries of social science. Only 'never mind'.

What was I typing so furiously, you might wonder? Which soon amounted to around fifty pages and had to be kept under lock and key in my girly, quilted wardrobe day and night. My Top Secret Sex Diary, of course.

Had human eye ever seen my Top Secret Sex Diary, I would have been removed from my happy home like a shot. For I knew nothing about sex save what I had read in my parents' weekly *News of the World*, hidden hastily beneath the settee cushions in the lounge. Whenever I was sure the coast was clear and they were happily ensconced at the Good Intent – O increasingly ironic handle! – I would lie wriggling on my right hand on the suitably named shag pile devouring exposés of vice girls, whips and two-way mirrors. These were the dog days of Janie Jones and Norma Levy, of Lord Lambton and Viscount Jellicoe; it wasn't the full-on Empire-shaking government-breaking orgies of *l'affaire* Profumo, but for a sleaze-starved pubescent pony it would do.

It remains an enduring and endearing feature of high-falutin', over-sensitive adolescent girls that we can countenance without the slightest trepidation a fantasy life involving an endless permutation of whips, dogs, vice girls, two-way mirrors and naked men in black rubber masks, but we would recoil and run screaming from a boy our own age just looking for a kiss.

Kevin Sweet was the first and last homeboy to taste my plush raspberry lips; in adolescence, as other girls refused at the shagging jump – girls who let themselves be fucked were soft, remember, not hard, and hard was all-important – but negotiated the snogging one, I literally wasn't having any. I had the most sure and awful feeling that if I ever kissed anyone I would not be able to stop myself from sleeping with them. Then, like as not, I would get knocked up. And then I would have to stay in Bristol. *To Live And Die In LA* sounded glamorously Chandleresque; To Snog, Screw and Spawn In Bristol seemed heart-breakingly naff. That it might be the title of the story of my life made me want to lie on the floor, kick my heels and scream. But more than that, it made me want to live like a bloody nun. Ambition is a far surer guarantee of female chastity than virtue ever was.

That Nicola Wyldbore-Smith. She may have had fancy things and diamond rings. In the summer of 1973, she may have had her place in the sun, or at least in 'Jennifer's Diary'. But at the age of thirteen I had one thing she'd *never* have.

Credit.

No, I lie. What I had was shoplifting. And shoplifting was, and remains, the greatest parasexual thrill known to man or girl. Girl, particularly.

Too hard for ponies, too smart for boys? Try shoplifting. Guaranteed to make your hair shine, your skin glow and your cycle regulate. And while you're at it, it's a lovely little metaphor for the poor working-class girl-child, sharp as a knife but only programmed for self-harming, determined to claw back just a little of what's been stolen from her class and its ceaseless labour.

Like most things in my clever little life, it started with a book. One day I was in a large Bristol department store called Fairfax House. (It's been pulled down now and there stands a large pink mall, as lovely and as corrupt as a wedding cake.) In my hand I held the latest Richard Allen, *Suedehead*, I believe. I was all set to pay my money and leave the building quietly.

And then what did I see? A naked female torso hanging from a rail. What red-blooded semi-Sapphic girl-child would not have been tempted? Though meant to be a caustic comment on how women's bodies are objectified, subjected and consumed by our society, to me it just looked so damn . . . *juicy*. Well, I was only thirteen and obviously hadn't been breastfed or anything nurturing like that. If I wanted to make up for lost time, who could blame me?

I looked around, my eyes sidling like snakes about to shed a skin –
as indeed I was: that of law-abiding Citizen Teen – and I slipped
both *Suedehead* and soft body into my satchel.

The warm internal glow that blossomed in my groin, like an
electric rose opening in fast motion, was a feeling as yet unknown
to me. It wasn't the screeching, hurtling ecstasy of a clitoral
orgasm; no, shoplifting is a lot more like the other kind. Which I
hadn't had yet, so couldn't then actually liken it to. But that's what
shoplifting feels like; a vaginal orgasm, all about possession and
enclosure and feeling full up with love. It never surprises me that
Shoplifting Shame, as the tabloids would have it, is largely the
province of menopausal ladies and wayward teens, all of whom are
more than likely missing a little something in that department, for
it is directly sexual and it is sexually insurrectionary; it is about
being the taker rather than the taken, the thief rather than the
swag. It may be anti-social, silly and intrinsically bad. But when
you are a working-class thirteen-year-old girl with a one-way ticket
– second class, at that – to nowhere, it feels like stealing back your
soul.

So *that's* how I got to read *The Female Eunuch*. It knocked me
sideways. But by the time I had grown up and become myself, and
it was re-released and the publishers asked me to write a new intro-
duction, I was pleased but I didn't do it. Like Fay Weldon –
'Women should wear high heels because it makes them easier to
catch' – and Nancy Friday – 'Women have got to ask themselves if
they are responsible for men's violence' – Germaine Greer has
become one of those women whom the menopause turns into hon-
orary men, full of envy and loathing for bouncy, flouncy young
women. And furthermore, even if it does sound petty as all-get-
out, when Miss Greer tried to pick that notorious Fuck-Me-Shoes
fight with my *amigo* Suzanne Moore, I was really glad I'd stolen
her rotten book and deprived her of her royalties. Moral: those
who act like royalty don't get one.

And so my first Career of Evil had begun. My head swam, bob-
bing above a veritable sea of puce tights, plum lipstick, maroon
tank-tops and Richard Allen books. I was rich; not especially in

possessions, because my parents had always been pretty generous. But I was rich because I was *doing* something; I was *being* something other than a schoolgirl, which I had always been lousy at anyway. It seemed to me that all I had ever wanted to do was make my own living and now in a way I was. I was keeping myself by my own wits and it felt like going home.

It was also one of the very few things, apart from my own thin, pale, cool right hand, which made me realise what sex would feel like. But not for long.

CHAPTER FIVE

Lemmings
in Love

What is love? If you or I had a one-pound piece for all the times we've heard someone say this – whether in their cups or on their uppers, on disc or at risk, married alive or as single as a Kraft cheese slice and just about as likely to get fucked in the foreseeable future – we'd be damned rich by now, wouldn't we? You'd have someone to turn over the pages of this book for you, more than likely. And me, I'd have someone to write it. But there, that's life; one day you're drinking the wine and the next day you're peeling the grapes and someone's calling you 'Beulah'.

I love love so much because it's such a surprise. Unlike money, or your career, which you can more or less make predictions and plans for after a certain point of success, love beggars belief – and the believer – more often than not.

We all know the naughty things love does. Laughs at locksmiths. Is the law. All's fair in it and war. Comes through the window wearing Mickey Mouse ears and carrying a sten gun. Is the mourner at every wedding and the jester at every funeral. Spends like a sailor on shore leave and takes no prisoners. One rainy afternoon in the February of 1995 I knew I was in love because I cleaned a girl's toilet, went out and bought her a sapphire necklace and then went back and gave her two hours of the best oral sex I bet she's ever had. I mean, go *figure*! You don't do *that* because you're in your right mind and you admire someone's handwriting.

Love blares 'Gotcha!' Love wears a bumper sticker that says 'My other car is a hearse'. Love says 'Give me the keys!' and slides into the driver's seat, snickering, because it knows that you don't know that it lost its licence ages ago for driving under the influence. It's extremely hard to describe; you don't like love, but you know what you like. And it's probably love wearing a different yashmak.

I've always considered it the biggest scream on earth when you get people like Barbara Cartland banging on about how backing 'romantic love' will lead to less sexual promiscuity. Of all the daft ideas! It is, of course, romantic love which leads directly to sexual promiscuity – or rather to sexual caprice, which sounds a damn sight less judgemental and is actually closer to what modern Western women practice – and a good thing too.

The Victorians and the prophets of the alleged 'Sexual Revolution' of the Sixties (called by one disapproving Seventies feminist 'The Great Sexual Appropriation', due to the fact that hippie girls usually ended up having sex with hippie boys as joylessly and powerlessly as their frat-pinned Fifties sisters did with letter-sweater jocks) had a good deal more in common than they knew. The Victorians wanted women to submit to the social authority of men; the Venals wanted women to submit to the sexual authority of men. They both basically wanted us to get down, albeit in different ways.

But women are subversive, disobedient creatures given half a chance, and romantic love is their weapon. A man will continue to have sex with a woman long after he has stopped loving her, just because she's *there*. But romantic love, and its supremacy in all moral matters, gives a woman *carte blanche* to withdraw sex whenever she wants to; 'I'm sorry, but I don't love you any more. I can't. I'd feel like a prostitute.' Heh heh heh.

That's why books about sexual technique are such a waste of time. And men with big penises, too. I used to believe that penis size was important and in the mid-Eighties I wrote a famous piece for *Arena* magazine called 'Where's The Beef'? It was fun at the time because agony aunts had been reassuring men for decades that 'size doesn't matter' and I thought it was about time men were given something to worry about, like women worry about so many of their body parts. But since then every dimwit sex columnist has started banging on about how *big* they like them, and I can afford to stand back and laugh and say that it really doesn't matter a damn. All that matters about having brilliant sex is being *in love* with that person – 'loving' them but not being in love doesn't count and is probably less aphrodisiac than hating them, by the way. Probably the most depressing ten words in the English language are 'I love you, but I'm not *in* love with you' – if anyone ever says that to me I'm suing.

Technique doesn't matter, size doesn't matter; if you aren't besotted by the face above you, nothing works. You look up at this handsome man, so well-hung, with such a great sexual reputation, whom a year ago you would have crawled along a corridor of glass shards to get shafted by and inside you yawn and you think, 'Oh *please*. Leave it *out*. Better still, *take* it out!'

For me, whenever ovaries come through the door, love goes out the window. I quite like being pregnant and I love my children, but I can't stand to hear anything to do with reproduction talked about. Even the word 'eggs' makes me feel queasy and I often think it's rude when you see them on menus. I remember when I first heard about ovaries I wanted to die. I became a homosexual instead, because it seemed to me that romantic love must be the exact opposite of any activity involving the ovaries.

This was when I was twelve. Not that I *did* anything about it; just sighed after my friends, read *The Well Of Loneliness* until I could recite it in my sleep – 'And that night, they were not divided!' – and developed an absolute phobia for boys. The *idea* that there were *these creatures* who could *activate your ovaries* and make you *into a hen*! – I gave them an extremely wide berth, I can tell you. If I was in the library and a boy got up and left, I would walk right the way to the other end to find a seat rather than sit on one still warm from his heaving hormones. Of course I knew the Facts of Life, but I didn't care. I wasn't taking any chances.

The Facts of Life. Is that the creepiest, most fatalistic description of sex you've ever heard, or what? 'Screwing', 'shagging' and 'nailing' are positively feministic and joyful compared with it. It's just so *grim*, isn't it? 'The Hard Facts', 'The Sad Facts' – facts just aren't user-friendly, are they? And when it comes to a thing like having sex with someone you're in love with, surely the most transcendent, magical experience we can have, short of flying on a magic carpet or finding a unicorn licking our toes when we wake up in the morning, what's nasty old 'facts' got to do with it? 'To love is to escape through one person the mediocrity of others' – I don't know who wrote that originally, although Charlotte Raven pretended she did in a letter to me in 1995. Then I saw it in a *Penguin Book of Modern Quotes*, so *she* can talk about lying, thankyouverymuch! But it's true, no matter who said it. If I want facts, I'll turn on Teletext. If I want magic, I'll make love to someone I'm in love with.

Chance would be a fine thing! I'd think gloomily as I glared adoringly at my friend, beautiful Nicola L in Biology. Her eyes by the light of the Bunsen burner glittered with the sedition of conformity and I longed to merge with her in the bubbling test-tube she held. She seemed more beautiful to me, with her swimming-pool eyes and silky, light-brown feather cut, than Beatrice, Laura and Helen put together. Ha, she probably thought that they were a new Sound Of Philadelphia girl group!

She felt my gaze and stared back into my green eyes – green for GO!, Nicola; green for GO! – with total attention to the subject in hand. Her lips parted and I smelt Juicy Fruit, for ever for me the scent of teenage lust. I waited, rapt, for her words.

'You got a girt big spot on your chin. You want to get some Ten O Six lotion.'

I smiled through my watery Bunsen tears while I screamed silently inside my head: No! I *don't* want to get some Ten O Six lotion and put it on my face! I want to get *you* and put you on my face, oh Nicola L from hell!

But no, no, no; as no as you can go. I was a blonde, twelve-year-old, emaciated-nymph beauty – and I stood about as much chance of getting on Nicola's tits in any but the irritating capacity as Brown Owl did. These girls, solely because of their indecent conformity, were straight as a die, wrong as a lie.

This being said, the signals they put out made life a complete nightmare of temptation, dashed hopes and denial. I believe that I have examined in my first chapter the strange and heart-breaking paradox that working-class girls are raised from babies to be the cleanest, pristinest, primmest little princesses who ever waved a scented hanky from a pink papier mâché castle and who never so much as *touch* themselves 'down there'. Then, on their twelfth birthday, with all the mercy and discretion of the Bad Fairy Carabousse herself, they are informed that *it is their duty* to let a sweating, fetid, drunken man, via a wedding band, hold them down one sad and sorry night and thereafter squirt a quantity of slime inside them. I mean, go figure *that*!

Little wonder that girls between the ages of twelve and sixteen – when it finally sinks in – find themselves in a more or less permanent state of hysteria, as they attempt to convince themselves that such a sorry end to their sugar-spun dreams is entirely logical; that they, little Lady Mucks of Sunnybrook Farm, were actually born to be a sexual Kleenex (ManSize). It's a shame there's not a Sexual Kleenex Barbie, complete with wedding night négligé and sheet with wet patch, to help the little darlings get used to it.

This hysteria and self-brainwashing takes many forms – becoming fixated on horses (obviously an attempt to acquaint oneself visually with the biggest, hairiest, ugliest dick around, so as to minimalise the dreadful shock on one's wedding night), or on teenage scream idols because they look so soft and fragrant and, anyway, you're never going to get to shag them but you're really *devoted* to them so you shouldn't really have sex with anyone else – it's a bit like being a nun with a Walkman.

Then there's ouija boards – like their mothers, and *their* mothers before them – which holds out some promise that there's life *after* this bastard dry (or rather wet) run, that *there's life without sex*! That's what draws women, as it nearly always is, to the supernatural time and time again; not life after death, but life after sex. (It's interesting that when men *do* get involved in the supernatural, it's to do with bending forks, not with being anti-matter from the waist down.) 'Teen Angel' sang some Bobby or Ricky in the American Fifties; he didn't know how right he was. Not only do teenage girls, at their best, literally *look* like angels – but they wish they were them, too: all wings, no strings. The idea of the teenage sex fiend Lolita is so far off the mark as to be tragi-comic. When girls do exhibit an actual sex drive, it signifies one of two things: infant rape, usually by a father, uncle or friend of the family – monkey see, monkey do – or an ill-chosen gesture towards rebellion. It's always sad when you see under-age girls having sex because they're angry about their putative lot in life as pram-pushing beasts of burden. Because of course it's exactly the thing that will only hasten their moment of execution. No one except another working-class woman will ever understand why schoolgirls have unprotected sex because they can't stomach the shrunkenness of their horizons. But believe you me, from in here it makes perfect sense. And no, you don't really want to see it from in here. Stay outside and count yourself lucky.

Being right at the bottom of the pressure cooker of sexual conformity and submission, while having the highest standards of romance and personal hygiene, completely scrambles the sexual–emotional thermostat of teenage girls, especially those of the prim and precocious working class. Middle-class girls can decide they want to study hard and get off sex that way; excuse me, we can't do that. Very early on, our emotional and social life *becomes* our career, and no mistake.

This drives us nuts, in one way or another. At the extreme end of the scale, the working-class recluse Karen Morgan, who died in 1995, simply stayed in her room for eight years from the age of twelve and almost persuaded her family, by force of her intelligence, to die with her as she slowly starved herself to death. A more photogenic hunger artist was Mandy Smith, the Muswell Hill Sleeping Beauty who hooked a millionaire in her thirteenth summer and spent the rest of her teenage life finding new ways to get a sick note to get her off sex, each one more complex than the last. 'Bill' Wyman, the paedophile – for that is what a man who has sex with a thirteen-year-old is – claimed that he was only allowed carnal knowledge of his eventual bride twice after they were married and that she took her mother on their honeymoon (sick-note writing obviously at a premium here); he should look in a mirror some time, and count himself lucky and blessed above all men that copious vomiting on the part of the indescribably lovely Amanda Smith did not render his gnarled fingers most unpleasantly 'sticky' every single time.

Really – what do such men expect? Do they think that teenage girls could ever – heh heh – *fancy* them, or something equally weird? But *whyyyyy*? It's perverted to fancy someone ancient and wrinkly and old enough to be your grandad. It's called gerontophilia; it's a real perversion, in the dusty old European sex books from the century's turn – it's necrophilia with a pulse and a Lamborghini. Yet the normalization of the sexual abuse of teenage working-class girls is so engrained in our culture that that culture's outrage over paedophilia seems slightly ill-sorted. A culture which prizes virginity and inexperience in girls as the ultimate sexual trophy leads the unbalanced man to the school gates; put Bill and Mandy in Regency dress and they could have stepped from the front cover of a Barbara Cartland novel.

I feel an especial regard and protectiveness towards teenage girls, because I was one when I realised that *something wasn't quite right*, that things were bad and dirty and loaded against us, punishing us for being so beautiful and yet so unused. That they would do their damned best to fuck us over in every way possible until we were as ugly and rancid as them, and only then could they sleep easy. The simplest way to fuck a girl over is sexually.

There must be a million cases like it, all judged and juried in their own neighbourhoods, but the Wyman–Smith case has been the most public and therefore the most easily referred to. Why has his subsequent marriage to an adult woman been featured in *Hello!* magazine without reference to his past? If a forty-seven-year-old man had repeatedly buggered a thirteen-year-old boy – albeit with that boy's consent and the consent of that boy's mother – would we still welcome him back into civilised society, or even into *Hello!*? I DON'T THINK SO!

And if not, why not? I'll tell you why: because our society, and every other, *hates* teenage girls – for their beauty, their lack of real heterosexual desire and their massive potential ability to bring down the mess of male misrule. Christine Keeler had been a teenager when she performed the acts that would bring down the government; Diana Spencer, Princess of Wales, was at heart for ever teen – shy, sly, fly, frozen in amber, frozen in anger – when she placed her pearly hands on the pillars of the English monarchy and pushed.

Paedophiles are, of course, famous for pointing their victims towards examples of the 'properness' and 'normality' of their torture – everybody's doing it! So we will never know how many child torturers pointed at society's acceptance of Bill Wyman's courtship, betrothal and casting off of Amanda Smith to justify their serial rapes. But I bet it was loads. Just *loads*. What a bloody field-day for the bastards! What a dirty great blank cheque! Put it *there*, Street Fighting Man! Way to go, *Je suis un Rock Star*! Let us hope upon hope that when you have a son with your very lovely grown-up wife, he gets buggered beyond belief by a real forty-seven-year-old platinum disc-dropper at the age of thirteen! And then let's see you complain! APOLOGISE OR BE SILENT!

Phew, got a bit carried away there! As I was wont to do, it must be admitted, when Nicola L put her arm around me and leaned in close in Biology, just to whisper in my ear that she 'fancied' Steven Jones. Well, she had a funny way of showing it, her lips lingering on my tender twelve-year-old lobe. Biology – I'd give her Biology!

Then there were those long sessions in the language lab when she'd squeeze herself into my booth and we'd become hysterical over the terminal ugliness of the German tongue. Language lab – I'd give her language lab! Language of *love*! Tongue? I'd give her . . . But of course I jest. I'm mugging now, not even *attempting* to replicate my lost love for Nicola L. Because I never, ever can. Once I've fallen out of love with someone, they become about as memorable as a sucked orange for me and I can never for a moment remember what I ever saw in them. Perhaps this is a necessary mechanism which the heart sets up in order to go through its future paces smooth as clockwork, but anyway it works for me. In love, a scorched-earth policy is the only one which makes it possible, paradoxically, for a thousand flowers of romance to grow.

Because love is a lemming. And its very death is what makes its continuing eternal existence possible. If we are to learn only one thing about romantic love which makes our lives less traumatic, it is not the usual tosh that people suggest. It is not that we should accommodate ourselves to filthy 'arranged marriages', thereby relegating human beings to the level of breeding stock. It is not that we should tolerate filthy 'open marriages', which take marriage to its logical and surreal bourgeois conclusion by insisting that *marriage is actually more important than sex* and must be preserved at all costs. It is, rather, that we should understand that the death of love is perfectly natural and no reflection whatsoever on the quality of the love itself. Why is longevity the last word? Who was the better pop group – the Sex Pistols, lasting three years, or the Rolling Stones, lasting three hundred? Exactly. (Incidentally, this rule holds true for everyone *in the world* except my parents. They've got to stay married *for ever*.)

Frankly, I don't remember any love except the one I've got now and the one I've got now said a clever thing when I asked him what it felt like when he – you know – that *thing* that happens towards the end of sex. He said, 'It's like being poured into your own body. It's like being made into yourself, new, each time.' Well, to me that's what love feels like. Becoming yourself, endlessly, without ever boring yourself. Boredom is just another word for not being in love.

So as it turns out I can't recall and display the love I lost, any of it. All for the best, I think. And all I really want to do with this book is not reveal, which is tacky, but warn, which is cool. I want to warn men that women hate them for the terrible things they've done and keep doing, and are getting to hate them more and more as time moves irretrievably on. In my youth, in the slippery 1970s, we expressed this by crying and clinging to our friends when drunk, and snogging our chief bridesmaid on our 'hen' night; right now, in the winter of 1996, I am looking at a survey of British women between the ages of fifteen and forty-five (a survey carried out by an advertising agency, which has little reason to invent such a user-unfriendly scene) which claims that less than one in three women feel that having a relationship with a man is 'very important'.

What does it say for you that we travel so fast now? That we are so faithless, blameless, shameless, yet still so very righteous in our sin? It says that you should pay attention. Just *pay attention*. And never, ever mistake me, King Girl, for some whole other person. Who died a long time ago.

I just turned in all honesty to my young companion and said to him, apropos of some minor nasty thing I'd been banged to rights for, 'I don't see why I should have to take the blame for everything I do!' He literally fell about. Then he suggested it might be a good title for this book.

I said it was too long. But I *will* enter it in my Book Of Evil Thoughts, which is what I keep instead of a poncey old journal or a girly little diary. If my Book Of Evil Thoughts gets long enough I may be forced to publish that, too.

CHAPTER SIX

Working-Class Zero

I'm not saying I was the Antichrist. Not even a minor demon. At Brownies I'd been a Sprite and I had a pretty hard time even living up to *that*. Capering around the large plastic toadstool at the end of an evening, I'd feel despairingly that my prancing lacked a certain Dionysian edge, unlike that of the small green embroidered creature on my breast-pocket badge, and I'd worry that somebody would notice and make me an Elf.

But as I skidded through my teens, my parents, teachers and friends conspired to make me feel like the true spawn of Beelzebub himself. Why? Because I was . . . difficult.

Importantly, I was difficult in a way that my would-be controllers could not categorize. I was not a hopeless teenage bed-hopper, seeking security from sex and ending up platform-soled and pregnant. I wasn't thick, frustrated by my struggles to 'keep up' with my class-mates. (What a scream! At the age of thirteen I was so widely read and quick-witted that I wouldn't have had any trouble keeping up with the Algonquin Round Table at the peak of their powers, let alone my slack-jawed contemporaries.) I wasn't an ugly duckling, whose problems could be solved with a dab of Clearasil and a diet sheet – I was, rather, a raving teenage beauty so conscious of her man appeal that I allowed an extra twenty minutes to walk to school, meticulously avoiding all building sites. Twenty minutes spent not lying in bed in the morning on a schoolday is a lot when you're fourteen.

Yet as the days counted themselves down to the starting block marked 'sixteen' – or rather, what would have been the starting block had I been *middle bloody class* but was actually, from where I was sitting, a lot more like a chopping block which would effectively separate me from my dreams for ever – I became a blob, spiritually if not physically, razor thin, shiv sharp and sad as Sunday.

I lay there in bed, ignoring my mother's repeated yells up the stairs to get-out-of-bed-you-lazy-cow and get a Saturday job. This entailed going to a hairdresser, sweeping dead locks into a pile and being handed a penny at the end of an eight-hour day; the cerebral equivalent of a training bra that it was considered desirable we working-class girls experience while still at school, just to make sure we were ground down nice and small and invisible to the naked eye when we were finally set free from our books to enter the exciting world of work. Maybe I was weird, but I was fucked if I was going to embrace my imminent death, let alone sweep up its pubes.

So now I know there's no point in me going to school, because it turns out to have been a spiritual slaughterhouse all along, there only to lead us little lost lambs to the altar, there to sacrifice us to husband and two veg and the whole filthy machine. I go instead, during school hours, to my grandmother's a lot; my grandmother, Eliza Burchill, née Skuse, is genuine working class, not like my parents, I like to snort to myself, who have been *bought* by three-piece suites and colour TVs. (Later, of course, when no longer blighted by that peculiar narrow-minded bigotry we call 'teenage', I realised that *people* buy three-piece suites and colour TVs, not the other way around.)

My gran lives in a modern block of flats in Barton Hill, which sounds posh but actually has a reputation of being extremely rough. Well, like the Shangri-La song said about a boy, it's good-bad but not *evil*, not like *Easton*. We Brislington babes lived in fear of Easton; a mean sprawl of council estates and sex pests (allegedly; none of us had ever been there), it was our definite no go area. Even as I grew to be a woman of the world, the word Easton could still strike fear into my sharply shod soul; when the singer Sheena Easton emerged, I used to sit and wonder for minutes at a time just why she'd named herself after such a place – why not 'Sheena Slum' or 'Sheena Sin Bin' if you really wanted to be so offensively punky? I finally cottoned that she came from Scotland and had never heard of the place. As you guessed correctly, I felt *really stupid*.

So I spend a lot of my days at my gran's flat, where she moved when the notorious Bridge Street was pulled down. These were large, crammed-together Victorian houses, three stories high, teeming with extended families; my father was brought up there with his three brothers and his sister Dolly (who was eventually to find shame and notoriety as the supplier of the monumental Golly at Noon rig-out) and he took my mother to live there after their marriage. It was while living there, my father away driving his lorry, that my gran and my mother became extremely drunk on port wine one night and awoke to find that *someone* – my mother timorously said my gran, my gran contemptuously said my mother – had made a lime jelly in the commode, set to livid green perfection. My mother was appalled, my grandmother – the main habituée of the commode – outraged. After that, the words 'jelly in the po' were all it took for my gran to get my mother whimpering. This is typical of Eliza. Like me, she combines both libertarian and Draconian moralities; that is, she thinks it's a real scream that my cousin Kim and I play truant so we can hang around her flat and steal Everton mints for her but if we got *caught*, on the other hand, she'd whip us and no mistake. Often, when irritated, she will threaten us with a white-hot poker. We would die for her.

When I'm not at my gran's, I spend a great deal of time concealing the fact that I'm having periods. Each month I hide the bloodied sanitary towels in my wardrobe and carry the key on me at all times. *I just can't give in*, for it would mean certain death and if my mother knew I was menstruating she would have *won* – girls stand a chance of escaping, whereas women do not. Each pad is sealed inside a plastic bag with a great deal of Sellotape, my very own bound and gagged little hostage to fortune, and when they start to breed, as is their wont and their will, and get to be uncontrollable, a veritable menstruation mountain indeed, I will leave them locked in, behind and run away to London at the age of fifteen to flee my shame. My parents will have to cut them out of the wardrobe and burn them in the garden at dead of night – an achingly poignant image if a vile one, the grieving parents making a bonfire of their runaway daughter's reluctant womanhood. Imagine how strange and lonely they must have felt at their nocturnal post. *Imagine*.

But I can't imagine anything now other than the pain of being myself, bright as a button and as easy to break, created only, it would seem, to slip into the shoddy workmanship, all threads and ends and unravelling, of the working-class woman's assigned buttonhole.

So I hang around my gran, as if that will make me an inviolate child again, and I collect my gory chorus of Kensington Gore-splashed cotton wool – and I stay in my bedroom, above all, the little prisoner in her padded cell, waiting for my death warrant – which round these parts we call a P45 – to be signed.

So pick a day, any day; I slam my door, throw myself headlong on to my bed and split a vast Brueghelian scream over the silent semi. ('Third lamp-post on the left after the Good Intent,' my father will tell taxi drivers. 'As if,' I say haughtily to Bambi, 'we were *dogs* marked by our favourite *urination* spot.') My scream shatters and cascades like a Methuselah of bad champagne and downstairs I just know that my parents are looking at each other quickly and then away, pretending not to have heard it. The dog whimpers in its sleep; it's having a bad dream. So am I. *It's called living in fucking Bristol.*

These days, of course, I can see the vast charm and appeal of Bristol, of my parents and of the dog, whichever dog he may be, to the strange point where, pulling out of Paddington and heading for Bristol Temple Meads, I actually sense a feeling of unmistakable *escape* from the cursed capital, whereas growing up I only ever imagined that Shangri-La lay on the other side of the tracks. I see, as I have said, what they had to put up with; this only child, conceived literally in all innocence, who quickly turned out to be about as comprehensible as a Martian or a Haitian, *no*, a Martian Haitian – Bringing Up Baby Doc. Today I feel sorry for them; at the time, beached on the shore of my own teenage sophistication, I hated them. And God, did I hate Bristol.

Not many famous people came from Bristol until the Bristol Sound made the world shiver; until the shimmering sorrow of Portishead and the majestic madness of Massive Attack explained me to myself. Before we found deliverance in our own backyard, we could count Cary Grant, two of Bananarama (the clever ones; that is, the ones who didn't have sexual congress with Dave Stewart) and Thomas Chatterton. The first three got out young; the last one topped himself at seventeen. In my fifteenth year, the burning question to me is *what took him so frigging long*?

I have spent the last three years now, school allowing, in my room with the purple curtains – purple for blood royal. Working-class blood royal! You know, the stuff that makes the middle class stage near-fatal car crashes so that they can get an armful of the joy-juice and *have some fun*. Ah, forget it – closed against the smell of muck-spreading, wafting in from the surrounding farms of Somerset, trying not to be in love with the by now irretrievable Nicola from L, sticking pins into my inept wax dolly of June Bolan and repeatedly playing the first bars of the 'Missa Luba Sanctus' as featured in *If*. . .. Occasionally I relieve the monotony by shaving off my eyebrows and replacing them with a thin line of red glitter, kept in place by eyelash glue. For this I am stripped of Monitor duties, which is a complete and utter con. I am truly Holly Golightly with a library ticket, except I don't want breakfast at Tiffany's. Because Tiffany's is a night-club downtown where Nicola L snogs boys and I avoid it like Plague Central.

In fact, my life is an exaggerated version of the usual rainbow of black magic, purple prose, blue Mondays, red mist and white lies which colours the life of any sensitive, too-clever-by-half (is there a phrase like this in any language other than bloody English? I brood moodily at least three times a day with the dutiful monotony of tooth-brushing) teen. And now, during said red mist attack in the school canteen (where part of the unwritten but immeasurably arcane initiation to the In Crowd – Girls – consists of sneaking out of the room with as much jam roly-poly as you can conceal, flushing it down the toilet and blocking up the drains so bad *that the plumber has to come out*. Ha! We could rival any swanky, homicidal Harvard sorority when it came to sheer, stylish, peer-group-pressure *evil*!) I have attacked a teacher – Mrs McIver – with a chair, after she ordered me to clear the table for a bunch of *boys*! And I have been suspended. Well, *cheap thrill*!

My father has threatened to smash all my records: 'Go on, then!' I weep, flourishing. 'And please don't forget "Goodbye Yellow Brick Road"! Which you bought me for Christmas! Which I *hate*!'

'Christ on a bicycle!' my dad retorts under his breath, already regretting his threatened and utterly uncharacteristic violence, even against vinyl.

'Yes, Dad! We *know* you are!' I finish cattily, before scampering up the stairs to my sanctuary. This is what they call an in-joke, which means it has been custom-made, with care and consideration beyond the call of duty, to injure one specific person, in this case the person I love above all others, who just so happens to ride a bicycle while all other fathers have cars. It's not poverty; it's not ecology; my dad just likes his bike. This is creditable; both because it means more money to be spent on *me* at Christmas and because it, um . . . the ozone layer.

Though of course we didn't know about the ozone layer then. We didn't have ozone. We had Buy Now, Pay Later. We had Big Fun (theory) which somehow always managed to boil down to Small Sad (practical). But that wasn't because we had a *spiritual* hole in our soul, like lots of why-oh-whiners are wont to say. It's because we were just growing into having a *political* hole in our soul.

Spiritual, for the working class, was covered – like a darn, like a soldier under fire – by Socialism, no problem. Political wasn't covered by anything and that's when the fingers of the drowning man lost their grip so painfully, so blatantly, so come-and-get-me stupidly. From fair shares for all to finders keepers; that was the politics I saw, from innocence to experience.

I saw, with my little maw, the raw foundations of a civilized society pulled down and most gleefully danced upon by Capitalism – only to have Capitalism turn around, reeling, in the party debris, asking why everyone was so savage, why they all wanted red meat. *Why couldn't people be, you know, civilized?* Well, by then you really had to laugh. *Because we tried, fuck you! It was called Socialism, and that was our last chance for civilization! And now we've got what you wanted! There is no society! Love it, or shove it!*

Really, you had to laugh. As I did, vilely, at my father's bicycle clips, which made his trousers so irretrievably *straight* in an age of flares. Later, in the closing act of the Nineteen Seventies, people will wear bicycle clips to make their flares seem straight. You really, really couldn't make it up.

Suspended! Up-ended! Which suits me *just fine*, as it gives me *even more* time to read books by Richard Allen and Oscar Wilde – I swing shamelessly now between *Suedehead* and *The Picture Of Dorian Gray* – pluck every single blond hair individually from my long pale legs (as I have read of the Princess Pignatelli doing, whoever *she* is) and admire the divine view in the looking-glass. It is the hottest summer of the century – the bonfire piled high and waiting, I cannot help but feel in my feverish state, for the kitten in the catacombs – and I am just about to turn sixteen. There's a drought. Officially. I'll say.

Nineteen seventy-six, so far, is an awful year for pop music, which obviously has until now seemed one of the very few reasons for staying alive. (Kill self Monday, won't know whether Sparks reached toppermost of poppermost Tuesday.) My heroes – Bolan, Bowie, Cassidy, Cooper – have run to fat and LA, every one, and whenever I see their ghosts on TV these days I look at them coldly with assassin's eyes.

Glitter, my bitter harvest, is dead, and the radio blasts me mercilessly with the most unbelievable, *literally* unbelievable, selection of songs: 'Convoy', 'Music Was My First Love', 'Silly Love

Songs', 'Jeans On', 'Devil Woman' and – for the love of Mike and the sake of Pete – 'Doctor Kiss Kiss'. Everywhere I look, it seems, Barry White and Telly Savalas and Demis Roussos are leering and groaning in my direction. No wonder I'm on Queer Street.

On 11 of December this year, the Nineteen Seventies will officially begin with the release of 'Anarchy In The UK' by the Sex Pistols, a little-known London beat group. But for now that rough beast is still slouching towards Manchester Square, waiting to be born, and I'm reeling under the mass attack of 'Fernando', 'Disco Duck' and 'S-s-s-single Bed'. To top it all, as if to rub my provincialism *right* in, rub my nose in it like some low-born mongrel who can hope for nothing more than a lonely life tied up outside the betting shop when he's supposed to be gambolling free, the *Wurzels*, a bunch of local showband yokels, are just hitting the singles chart with a glut of ooo-arr innuendo pop such as 'I Am a Cider Drinker' and 'I've Got A Brand New Combine 'Arvester'.

This is the final insult. This is adding insult to injury. This is adding injury to, like, being born with both metaphorical legs jammed behind your ears, trussed up like the Christmas turkey and signed-sealed-delivered to rotten, stinking society, I think with my usual gift of cool evaluation and native understatement. I lie on my s-s-s-single bed with the curtains drawn as per, reading Dorothy Parker with my Miners Plum Gone (my lipstick! My very *lipstick* is a metaphor for my lousy life!) lips moving, dreaming of the very wettest of girl's kisses and the very driest of Martinis – and I am mocked by muck-spreaders and scrumpy-swillers.

The hushabye-thighed, faraway-eyed girls on my beloved Biba posters – Maudie James and Stephanie Farrow – gaze down pityingly at me. For I am as beautiful as they, yet they know I am never to know a boa or go to Goa. Never mind, though. My platform shoes may be stuck in the shit of Somerset, but my head is in the art-deco clouds of Thirties Manhattan. Softly I hum, to the tune of 'Home On The Range':

> 'Home, home at the Algonquin
> Where the *fin de siècle* bons vivants play

Where never is heard
A one-syllable word
And no one mispronounces pâté.'

So I sprawl there, catcall there, sucking my hair and sorting my Cocktail Sobranies, my precious ones, my precious, myself. There are basically only three things I want to do: be famous, sleep with a Jew and take drugs – and then, God, you can kill me. Take me. Leave me. Whatever. But please God, not till then.

Fat chance! The scrumpy-drinkers sing. I scowl, select a mauve Sobranie and fire it. Beam me up, Dottie . . .

When I see myself, I see myself walking away. From the tearful slamming doors of my teenage to the moonlight flits from my marriages, I see myself forever leaving. I'm not particularly proud of this. But that's the way it is.

Other people dream of leaving; I leave so I can keep on dreaming and never be drawn down into the quicksand of the everyday, of the life less lived. But most of all I leave because I never feel as much at home as when I'm closing the door on it.

I started on my career of leaving when still legally a child. When I was fifteen, my life came to a head; a big, throbbing poison pustule made up of equal parts boredom at my school situation, dread at the thought of the seat at the conveyor belt of my mother's old alma mater – Mardon's Son & Hall, the cardboard box factory – no doubt being saved for me, and the terminally squalid fact that the sanitary towels in the wardrobe were threatening to up sticks and take over the entire household. After two years, my pathological shyness meant that I had *still* not informed my parents that I had achieved the menarche. There was only one thing for it – leave town, but fast . . .

I had often fantasized about running away – like suicide, like old money, it was something to fall back on when teenage traumas got too tough. I had often packed my parents' shabby suitcase with the things that soothed my soul, the satin and tat and gymkhana books, and wept over it when a few grains of sand reminded me of childhood idylls at Butlin's, now seeming so far away, buried in the blood and tears of your typical humid female adolescence. But at the last moment I had always bottled out – lost my nerve completely and run around frantically unpacking everything, especially the emergency cash I had taken from the box under my parents' wardrobe, before I heard my father's key in the door at six. For a period after that I would feel very weepy and relieved, and very much in love with my parents. Running away concentrates the mind – and heart – wonderfully.

But I knew that my life couldn't go on as it was. For a long time now, since pubescence, I had felt as though I was in exile – that's the only way to describe it. Yet how could I be – there I was, living in the house I had lived in all my life? I was in exile, obviously, from the life not yet known; the life which was meant for me. The life, dammit, which some other bright working-class girl might spy at some spiritual Bring And Buy sale, try on for size and take away with her. *Some other girl might end up walking around with my life on!*

As the long summer holidays of my fifteenth year loomed, I decided once and for all that I must *make* myself go – go now, or forever rest in peace. My mother gave me money to buy a new coat. I kept it and stole a coat from a girl in my class called Wendy Huntley. If she writes to me, I will send her both my apologies and the money I owe her. By the way, Wendy, the arms were too short and you'll be glad to hear I looked really rough in it. It was a natty little grey tweed Crombie-style number, though not cut for a long-stalked lovely like myself.

So those school holidays didn't pass in the usual haze of boredom, euphoria and non-specific desire, but rather started each day with the lurching nausea of what I can only describe as stage fright. For I was, I knew now, about to step out into the world and I had no doubt whatsoever that the spotlight would shine hard and fast on me.

There was just one more thing I had to do to be sure of my successful passage into the real world: I had to disguise myself. Hair seemed the obvious, not to say the only element of myself I could

possibly change the colour of without drawing undue attention –
remember, I was a veteran of the Golly At Noon wars.

The Sunday night before I was due to return to school I crept
into the bathroom with a box of blond bleach. Half an hour later
my silky golden-brown pelt resembled a stick of vanilla candy floss.
I gaped at myself. I saw a stranger, but then I *always* saw a stranger:
someone's daughter, someone's schoolgirl, someone's *child*, of all
the cheeky assumptions, had always been the interloper in the
looking-glass. This ur-blonde *thing* was certainly no exception.

Well, I'd done it now. Which meant *I'd have to do it now.* I
wrapped a towel around my head turban-style and sauntered down
to the living-room, trying to pass for normal. Whom was I kidding? But on the other hand, I suppose my parents were so used to
my abnormality that nothing surprised them any more.

'I'm going to bed now. To be fresh for tomorrow.'

''Night, love.' They didn't even look up. I could have gone in
there disguised as a Nubian boy, complete with top-to-toe body
make-up and an aged brown banana for a penis and they wouldn't
have looked up from *The Onedin Line.* Which was just the way I
wanted it. I closed my bedroom door on a dreary world for what I
sincerely hoped was the last time and slept the sleep of the just for
the first time in my life. The just-about-to-be-born, that is.

In the morning, as soon as my parents had gone to work, I went
to my packing with a will. My suitcase was heavy, but there was
nothing else for it; my record collection must come with me. Of
course I wasn't sure if there was a hi-fi or even a humble Dansette
where I was going – but to leave behind Ziggy Stardust, Alladin
Sane, Electric Warrior and their friends Kimono My House,
Stranded and For Your Pleasure was not even a consideration.
How would they live without me, or I them? The fact that I
thought this of my records rather than my parents now strikes me
as surreal in the extreme. At the time it seemed as natural as
breathing.

And so the lanky but not graceless blonde teenage bombshell,
weighed down by the considerable weight of at least twenty long-
playing records, grabbed the emergency cash from under her

parents' wardrobe in her hot little hands and walked out of her father's house as casually as she could manage. My suitcase was heavy, but my heart was light. I walked towards Temple Meads, waiting to be born.

Remember that I was no ordinary child. I would never have dreamed of being an ordinary teenage runaway either, ending up on drugs in a brothel. Truth to tell, the idea was quite hideously attractive to a highly charged virgin like myself. But I was sensible enough to know that such a choice would in some way signal the end of my life. What I wanted more than I had ever wanted anything was for my life to *begin*.

I didn't go to London in search of fame or fortune or sex or drugs. (Not *this* time, anyway.) I went there simply because I no longer felt like a child – thus, living with my parents and going to school felt freakish and silly. In recent years we have seen the phenomenon of the grown man who somehow disguises himself as a schoolboy and wangles his way back into secondary school in order to live his teenage years all over again. Invariably, he is a roaring success. This makes me think that some people are suited to school and some people are not, regardless of age. I was not – it was that simple.

For I was born to be alone and it is impossible to be alone in a school more than it is anywhere else. Even in prison you are allowed, indeed encouraged, to take time out inside your own head – at school, this is wool-gathering. Truth to tell, I was a lonely little soul and by some dark magic this loneliness only stopped hurting – became instead a feeling of absolute satisfaction – when I was physically alone. That's why, more than I like anything – more than sex, or drugs, or money – I like walking away.

It was the sheer spiteful thrill of this which stopped me from feeling any hint of fear throughout that two-hour journey to the capital. I sat there in second class – as God is my witness, I'll never go second class, or even Weekend First, again! – and seemed to hear the blood rushing in my ears as the sea rushes within a shell. Truly, I was *The Cruel Sea*; truly, I was *The Deep*, my heart as cold as Davey Jones's locker.

I couldn't read; reading was what you did on journeys and this was the first time I *wasn't* trying to get somewhere – I was there at last, where I wanted to be, moving towards London by the minute. This was, at last, my Overture and Beginners. All I could do was lean forward in my seat, urging the hot metal beast on, look at my glittering eyes – wicked eyes, it occurred to me suddenly – in my mirror and laugh.

Yes, laugh. I don't often come over all Nietzschean – I'm a right little angel of mercy on a daily basis – but when I'm walking away is the one time I tend to. I look at people and despise them for staying – especially women, whose very faithfulness will more than likely at some point encourage some man to dump all over them. I know it's wrong, but there ain't a damn thing I can do about it. I look at people and I laugh at them because I know, I just *know* they're playing it straight.

The worst time was when I left my first husband for my second; I stood on Billericay railway station waiting for the train to whisk me away back to London and life, twenty-four and strong as steel, and I literally wanted to run amok pushing all the old ladies and housewives on to the track, just for being so *straight*, so *good* and yet so depressed, when I was so full of life and so *bad* and so happy. Instead I just laughed at them, snarling, my lips peeling back from my teeth like the beast I was. (And am, someone said. Quite right, Charlotte R.) No doubt they'll have the last laugh, eh? But on the other hand, I think we both know who'll have had the best fucking time *ever* by the time we all turn up our toes.

Save yourselves, you bloody fools! I wanted to cry. Save yourselves, or people like me will skin you alive. Well, I know it's bad. But on the other hand, it's the truth. And the truth, as we're all told, is a wonderful thing and shall make us free.

No one was ever freer than me by the time that mechanical voice – truly sounding like the voice of God to my blasphemous teenage ears – announced that we were about to pull into London Paddington. In slightly less than two hours I had shaken off fifteen years of a provincial upbringing devoted to preparing me for the fact that mine was a life which would without doubt be lived in the quietest possible style my friends and family could manage, and that all going as planned, my name would occur in the newspapers only twice: when I married and when I died. Really, I thought now, wild-eyed and snarling with joy as I hefted my sorry suitcase from the rack, why didn't the women of my home town just have the two announced as one and save unnecessary expense? Really!

Remember, I didn't *feel* like a child; I didn't feel illegal. Add that to the fact that now I really did feel unstoppable and my first plan of action was understandable; I went straight to the YWCA and found a bed among the slender, sad provincial typists and bouncing foreign students. I was, after being in London for one hour, made totally aware what at least seventy-five per cent of the adult male population wanted to do to me and I certainly didn't plan on letting them have their way.

London was at this time quite awash with Arabs and I dare say that to their eyes, bloodshot with Chivas Regal and late-night casinos and Bunny Girls' bobtails, a teenage blonde with legs up to her boy's behind and a skirt which would barely have passed muster as a cummerbund wandering dazedly around the streets of the West End and beyond appeared to be just looking for trouble. But I wasn't; I was looking for, and finding, the London I had seen on screen.

I'm in London. LONDON! I felt like a little metal sphere bouncing around a big bright pinball machine. KERCHING! – all the buses are red! KERSPACK! – all the girls are thin! There's the King's Road, down which Julie Christie swung in the sunlight of the endless Chelsea morning! There's Powis Square, where Turner tempted Chas in *Performance*! There's the Post Office Tower, where the girls had the fight in the revolving restaurant at the end of *Swinging Time*! AND ME RIGHT IN THE MIDDLE OF IT! THERE IS A GOD AND HE WEARS A PLASTIC UNION JACK POLICEMAN'S HELMET!

So I wasn't looking for trouble; I considered my life in Bristol to have been all the trouble I'd ever need and dead boring to boot. And if I had been, *they* certainly wouldn't have been the sort of trouble I was looking for, being far uglier and smellier even than the boys of Bristol. Good God, I thought, increasing my platformed pace as the nth Arab that hour growled and rattled his trouser-pocket change at me, I didn't spend fifteen years keeping myself pure of the men of Somerset county just so I could fall into the straw with some sweaty, sour-smelling camel-shagger.

(And by the way, there's no use yelling racism. If a man behaves in a sexist manner – if he's not gender-blind with women he doesn't know, if he harasses them on the street, if he turns what should be a civilized city into a gauntlet – he forfeits his rights to my colour-blindness. If he doesn't like it, tough testes. The answer is simple: *Do as you would be done by*.)

Not that I hated foreigners by any means; foreign girls, I've always found, are just my speed – they feel like strangers in town, too. The first week I was there, an Egyptian girl student in my dormitory climbed in late one night through the window, after I'd opened it for her, sat on my bed and told me that the YWCA was a total rip-off and the girls too prim. (It must have been my hair which signalled unChristian floozie to her.) We were going, she informed me, to a hostel in the Gray's Inn Road – 'Where you can get in any time you feel, OK!' (Nabila always ended questions with an exclamation mark) – and during the day I would work at the chemist's shop on King's Cross station where she moonlighted weekends. ('Cash in hand, which suits you, because you're not of age, are you!')

Too right. This was an offer too good to refuse. But Nabila and I made big eyes at each other when we set down our bags in our new dorm – even the walls looked as though they had an itch they couldn't scratch. But suddenly our faces cleared as a girl stood up and came towards us.

I've never been one for the 'They Smile And The Sun Comes Out' line; too often, and embarrassingly, it's used by white music journalists about black musicians. But when I was fifteen I met someone who could perform this extraordinary cosmological feat. She was an Australian girl called Judi Flanders – 'Judi with an Eyyyyye', she would say and her eyes, long and Chinoise, would crinkle up at her own pretension; in Australia, spelling Judi with an I defined pretension.

Australia was a *bad* country, Judi told me that first night. 'It's no accident Germaine Greer was Australian!' Yet in Judi I saw all the weird, outlaw, reactionary, contradictory splendour of that country, which finds its finest expression in its wild colonial girls. Judi was a Hard Girl – glamorous, chaste – but she had a soft centre. I never told her I was a runaway but she guessed and made it her business to protect me from my own nation's capital. It was as though she'd been sent all the way across the world to look after me.

Judi was a Temp and ever since then I have found the word Temp to be by far the most exotic job description I have ever heard, far more so than the accepted shimmer of model or actress. What are you? – I'm *a temporary*. Well, join the club; so am I. I'm your Temporary Girl. She earned good money, but she sent it all back to Australia for reasons she was typically too modest to divulge.

I was quickly selling scent in the chemist's on King's Cross station; I was good at my job, being young and pretty and innocent-looking once my hair had been dyed back to normal on the insistence of the shop manageress ('Excuse me saying this, luv, but you'll be selling scent. Not a quick shag. You look like a baby hooker'). Businessmen heading back North after a week's business (dirty, no doubt) in the sinful smoke would be in the mood to spend a lot of money on their wives waiting suspiciously at home in Alderley Edge and Wilmslow and they would want to know what it smelled like on an actual woman. Well, I wasn't *strictly* one yet but I was happy to oblige by spraying my wrist and offering them a quick sniff. I sold an awful lot of scent that way; truth to tell, I think I might have missed my true calling.

I worked a twelve-hour, six-day week; money in hand, no tax, no National Insurance, no questions asked. It was a lot of money for those days – sixty-five pounds in 1975, as I remember – but the complete and utter bastard who ran the Gray's Inn Road hostel had cottoned on, with the few words of English he spoke, that we were all some sort of illegal and charged us an arm, a leg and an attempted molestation once a week for the privilege of staying under his skanky roof. But we were wise to his ways and all stuck together whenever the rent was due. It was just like a *Gold Diggers* film from the Thirties – only without the gold.

But what there was, was a whole lot of Girl Power – except it wasn't called that back then. In fact, what we think of as an attitude to life, love and lipgloss originating with the Spice Cadets actually had its generous-minded genesis in the glorious, gutsy dames of the Thirties and Forties cinema – Ann Sheridan, Barbara Stanwyck, Ginger Rogers, Eve Arden, Celeste Holm, Ava Gardner and Lana Turner, ever ready with a dozen quips from their ruby lips with which simultaneously to put down a man and buoy up a sister. There was always an unspoken assumption among such women – which the Spice Girls carry on admirably – that while the earth may well move with one particular boy, the breed on the whole are a bad lot, forever looking at a woman's legs with a view to kicking them away from under her. Men are there to be taken – not taken as in taking your punishment, as soppier women seem to believe, but taken as in take for a ride. And then, preferably dumped unceremoniously with their trousers down and the ignition missing its keys miles from anywhere on the highway between Fool's Paradise and Lonesome Town.

Or rather, left staring wildly about them in the pubs, clubs and hotel lobbies of Wild West Wonderland while Judi and I exited in an agony of laughter after blagging that final insulting fifty-pence piece to tip the toilet attendant with. It was September, an Indian summer, and when we weren't working for our pay we always seemed to be running somewhere; and it always seemed to be night, deep, hot night. French-Algerian Dominique, Canadian ice-blonde Paula, Aussie Judi and little me, the girl from Nowhere-upon-Avon; running alleys, down fire escapes, the whole heaving summer-night city acting as our ever-changing stage and all the men upon it merely players struck dumb by our pitiless determination to *have a good time, all the time.* And playing in my head continuously was a reggae song that was a hit that summer: 'I've got one more silver dollar . . . but I'm not gonna let them catch me, no, not gonna let them catch the Midnight Rider . . .'

Looking at the alleged It Girls now, it strikes me what a tame time they seem to be having compared with the average bevy of shopgirls and typists from time immemorial to this very day. For a start, they're over-age and overpaid, and the police aren't after them; and what kind of real fun can you say about that, eh? So far as I can tell, to be an It Girl is to live the life of a bored trophy wife with no visible husband – all the time the endless networking with men and women old enough to be your parents, all the posing for the camera, all the moribund middle-aged interest in, yawn, shopping, dieting and keeping fit. For that is what the stupidly named 'working out' is: naff, old-fashioned 'Keep Fit' by another, more acceptable name. You 'work' when you're earning a living, *not* when you're touching your toes or cocking your leg. That's not work, that's pissing your life away. And waste precious life on that endless grind, when there are drinks to be drunk, food to be scoffed and slappers to be saveloyed? I don't *think* so. It is a well-known fact that acquiring a husband makes a woman officially and spiritually middle-aged; lacking them – a fact which they never cease complaining about – makes it inexcusable for the It Girls to be so boring.

As for me, my nights as a London butterfly were the best fun I'd ever had – *and* I got to keep my clothes on. Which notable achievement made me glare with righteous anger at the policeman who picked me up, answering to a description of a fifteen-year-old Bristol runaway, found fifty pounds in cash in my cheesecloth pocket and asked me if I was 'on the game'.

'No I am bloody well *not* on the game!' Beat. 'But if I was, I'd have earned a lot more than *that*.'

The man who walked into the police station in West End Central to take me home looked at least a dozen years older than the man whose house I'd left eight weeks before. But he had the good grace to smile wearily when the pretty blonde policewoman told him that he should be proud of his daughter: 'Mr Burchill, there aren't many girls of Julie's age who could keep out of trouble *and* support themselves the way she has. The manageress at the chemist's said she was the best, most hard-working girl they had . . .'

'Come on, girl.' He stood up. 'Let's go home.'

Well, the long and the short of it – and it was quite short, but it seemed very long – is that I was taken home and sent back to school for a year until I could leave legally, and from there to a technical college for a year to do my O Levels in a more liberal, shall we say, environment. And from there no doubt to a teacher training college and thence to some other place and hung by the neck until dead or married.

My parents, teachers and contemporaries treated me politely and distantly, like a paying guest, from then on; I liked it a *lot*. Because I had proved I *was* different, that I *didn't* belong there. I belonged out in the hard, cold world, earning my hard, cold living to my hard, cold little heart's content.

And when, as luck would have it, the *New Musical Express* stepped smartly between me and teacher training college and I retraced my steps to London, legally this time, I felt I hardly missed a beat; I was walking away, again, and it couldn't help but feel like home. He who is not busy walking away is busy planting one foot in the grave.

I like to think I've changed a bit, now, and that I won't keep running for ever. Keeping on running when you've got arthritis and a Zimmer frame somehow just doesn't have the desperado glamour of being a teenage runaway. But still the allure of lonesomeness, the pure equation of the solitary, sings its siren song to me, a song heard long ago, probably in my lonely cradle, and never quite forgotten as an ideal for living.

Even now I can be walking down the street with the boy or the girl I love more than anyone outside of my immediate family, and I look at them and they're so beautiful and clever, looking at me with the boldest eyes and the sweetest smile, and the sky is blue and the smell of my swimming pool is on my skin – and I feel that something is terribly, terribly wrong.

And that something is not as it should be.

And then I realise what it is.
I'm not alone.

A few things lighten my darkness, even through my purple curtains. One is the thought of suicide, which is what sensitive teens
get instead of a trust fund. It is always there, the final, velvet,
roped-off area, when life gets too loathsome, swinging softly in the
sad cul-de-sac of my inner-city mind like a sweet chariot or a safety
net; a great comfort to fall back on, even better than old money.
Because *I earned this myself*.

The second is the One Good Teacher who plays Fairy
Oddmother to every lucky Bad Teen; you can have no-good
parents and just about do OK, but if you have no-good teachers
you have (a) my sympathy and (b) no chance whatsoever, for
teachers, like friends, should be God's apology for relatives. Mr S
is a handsome young head – English teacher, natch; inspirational,
life-saving Maths teachers are about as rare as a female orgasm in
Eire – who feels that to put me in a factory, like my mother and her
mother before her, would be akin to putting a peacock in a goldfish
bowl. Or a goldfish in a sardine tin. One that you can't even open,
what's worse, because the key keeps breaking off. No kidding, as I
approach sixteen, that's *just* what my life feels like. On a *good* day.

Mr S and I are in love, it would appear, gazing moodily at each
other across the thick heads of the lumpenclass, two pale and sarcastic outsiders together, but it must be together alone, sadly, as I
have taken a silent vow of heterosexual chastity for the duration of
my stay in the open prison we call home sweet home. Too many of
my ex-friends' lives are about to end in pregnancy at sixteen –
working-class women still die in great numbers due to childbirth:
they just die in a different way, is all – and I'm too young to die. I
think of the ironic, poncey name for coming: *le petit mort*. Ha!
Working-class girls *cut out the middle man*, Mr Climax whoever-
he-is-when-he's-at-home, and go straight to the chase. *Le petit
mort* becomes *le petit* mortgage. And it's not bloody glamorous or
easily translated into Frog, let me tell you! Pretty soon Mr S leaves
to write his book on William Blake, but I've got what I wanted

from him. A second opinion – from a *book-learning man*, no less, to my redneck Lolita! – on my *specialness*. (All those short stories about bad sex and alienation he thought were so good; I can't believe I copied them out of *Cosmopolitan*. The state of my ethics, even then!)

The third thing is my *New Musical Express*, a miracle which drops through the letter-box once a week. I'm always surprised it doesn't set the carpet on fire, like it does my brain. There are few minor beauties more inspiring than a magazine whose time has come and by the mid-Seventies the *NME* was riding the crest of the perfect wave. A bleached, beached beauty of some sixteen summers and seventeen sorrows, treading water in the quicksand shallows of my hope-murdering backwater, it might seem unlikely that I will catch it. But I do.

Surf's up. And so is my waiting.

CHAPTER SEVEN

I'm Off

We're going to stop for a commercial break for my first employer here, but I hope you'll bear with me. This is where the second act of my life begins, so please ignore the apparent tawdriness of the fixtures and fittings.

My pop life was nasty, brutish and not quite short enough for my liking, even though I was in and out under three years. Compared to most of the middle-aged foot-and-nose soldiers who labour for a pitiably small return for the music press, I was a complete and utter fly-by-night and therefore probably not to be trusted to report professionally on matters rockist as I never went On The Road with Thin Lizzy on three separate occasions. But I'll do my best to tell the truth, though I certainly won't tell all of it. Truth, especially when it comes to matters of the heart and of the loins, is like food: best to leave a little on the side of the plate for Mr Manners. No one likes a lady (or a gent) who goes at the truth like a piggy at its trough, thank you! If you want a Kiss and Tell, go and buy a book by someone like Blake Morrison or Paula Yates. Not by a proper writer, like what I am.

It seems implausible and somewhat risible now, but in the period between 1972 and 1980 the *NME* was a lifeline – the World Service of Hip – for the scattered tribe of Neurotic Boy Outsiders of all three sexes isolated far and wide throughout the British Isles and beyond. Years later I was to meet an NBO from New Zealand, of all places, who described that sensation as well as any of us: 'Can you imagine being fifteen and just sitting on this *rock* at the end of the world . . . and then suddenly every week this *paper* starts to arrive telling you what the New York Dolls are doing. *And for an hour you actually feel as though you're all on the same planet!*'

I started reading the *New Musical Express* at the age of twelve, due to its coverage of the career of Marc Bolan – definitely beyond the call of duty, though not of beauty – and stayed with it even after he grew fat and my love grew lean. I had never heard most of the music they talked about, of course – obviously they had made the New York Dolls up. Come on! They're junkies, with bouffants, and they wear red leather and play in front of a hammer-and-sickle backdrop. Yeah: in my wildest, wettest teenage dreams, no doubt, *but nowhere else*! *And* they probably imagined that the Hues Corporation were arms manufacturers. I am well aware that I am the only soulgirl in the history of the world who has read the *New Musical Express* religiously – like a fool, washing my hands *before* I read it, rather than after, when they're covered in ink – for four years solid, but I *don't care*. Because these people whom I will never meet writing about this music I will never hear makes me feel *not alone*, which is by now quite a novelty. They make me feel *less lonely*, in a way that discothèques and black music and my girlfriends do not any more; in fact, all these I have loved only seem to conspire to make me lonelier these days. I can no longer pass for normal; it's a fair cop, guv. Nicola L and her catcalling crew melt away like little hard, sad ghosts, mirages in Trevira suits and two-tone shoes, little ghosts waiting to die twice, once and for all.

But, thank God, at least this would appear to be the year in which the Sixties are finally shutting up shop: Wilson gone, Mao dead, Patty Hearst cornered, Britain trotting off to the IMF like a kid with a big black 'See me' in its homework book. I am thrilled that dishy, saturnine Jeremy Thorpe is a homosexual, though no one else seems very pleased by the news. (My friend Daniel commented poignantly on the apparent innocence of my time, the Seventies, on seeing his first picture of Thorpe, before his unmasking, as leader of the Liberal Party, in a public place swishing an evening cape and smoking from a cigarette holder: 'And *nobody knew?* But he's got "Bring me my catamite!" written all over him!')

I am in love with Nadia Comaneci (for her perfection) and John Stonehouse (for his imperfection). I'm glad that the Sixties are finally finished, but impatient for the Seventies to start; I don't know where or when that will be, but I fully intend to be there. Even if I've got to bunk off school and take an AwayDay to wherever they're going to start. Because it sure as hell won't be in bloody *Bristol*. No, we'll probably get the Seventies by about 1985, if our past achievements in popular culture are anything to go by.

In the churches of Somerset, now Avon county – 'Ding dong! Avon calling!'; not to me, it's not! – they pray for rain. In my room, during that long hot summer, so do I. *A flood*. Anything to stop me going to school. 'I tell you it's *killing* me, Mother! Why is it all right for me to be *murdered*, but not to commit suicide?'

'Because it's the *law!*' the poor woman moans.

'What – me being murdered? By society? Slowly? For being different? Thanks a bundle! *I didn't ask to be born, you know*! Why didn't you get rid of me then instead of waiting sixteen years? *If I was going to die anyway?*'

Hell, I was sixteen. I have no guilt. You *think* like that. If you're still breathing, still dreaming of leaving.

I read in my *NME* about this Americaine, Patti Smith, who confirms for me Mary McCarthy's line about American women being the third sex, from the lips of Lakey's lesbian baroness. I see this picture of her standing up against a wall with a jacket slung over her shoulder. For those of us who saw that black-and-white photograph in 1976, it remains as endlessly iconic as Marilyn over the grating or the England 1966 squad over the moon. It was proof of perfection – not as something dead and gone and preserved in a case, but perfection as something ordinary, almost everyday, if you were smart and hard and soft enough. I don't see perfection like other people see it, in a respectful, self-loathing, nothing-to-do-with-me sort of way; I see it as a racket we have all got a chance to get into, if only we choose our moment wisely.

When I finally get my hot little hands on her record, *Horses*, I am deeply moved; to say the least. So deeply moved, in fact, that after first playing it I have to send my clothes to the dry cleaners and smoke a Sobranie. Pink, as I remember.

I fell out of love with Patti Smith before the year was out, when I met her in her dressing-room at the Hammersmith Odeon and she tried to procure me for one of her horrible hippie band – wham, bam, *no* thank you, ma'am! But by then, of course, I didn't give a flying frigadoon. Like Mr S, whose fine facial hair she too could boast, she'd done her bit for me; played John the Baptist to my career's Christ, in fact. Because a week or so after hearing her record – and it *was* a record, a big, beautiful babe whose sleeve you could stick on your wall and snog and rub against your hard-nippled breasts, not some stingy little tape or CD you'd be lucky to get an inch of fun out of – I spy an advert in the back of my *NME* for a *hip young gunslinger*. I thought – eww, macho cowboy imagery, they must be really sexually inadequate up there. Then I thought – I can do that.

I am singularly thin and pale and profoundly, lividly young. My youth stands out on me like welts, stinging, and I wear my zits like medals. I'm *young young young*, and I'm going to milk the cashcow for all it's, all I'm, worth. Disregarding Baby's First Typewriter, I wrote my *Horses* review by hand on bad school notepaper, torn and jagged just like me, a word or two here and there deliberately mis-spelt. I was stage-managing myself even then, even before I got on to the stage. In ten years' time, this sort of caper will be called a 'career move'.

It's about as drooly and libidinous as only a virginal sixteen-year-old can be, and it certainly gets *their* blood running. Oh, I just thought of a brilliant line I should have used: 'Every little girl loves something hard and fast and diamond hard between her legs, something that's going to give her the ride of her life, to infinity and beyond. That's why every little girl loves *Horses*.' Eww, smutty! But you get my drift.

I'm Off

I suppose the Sapphic ravings of a sixteen-year-old Somerset schoolgirl stood out considerably, considering the *NME*'s reader profile – very male, very twenties, very straight. I'll give you a working definition of straight – really boring, stupid, straight, shall I? Oh all right then, you've twisted my arm. Straight to me isn't someone who doesn't take drugs; they're fine by me, so long as they don't spoil other people's fun. No, straight is someone who buys drugs *and saves them for later*. For a special occasion. For Friday night. That's what I imagined my fellow putative gun-slingers being like – Hip Squares, the lowest of the low. 'How dare you suggest I sling my gun now – it's not even High Noon!' Like that.

And I was bloody right. Sebastian Faulks was one of the 15,000 applicants for the job; excuse me, in which solar system was Sebastian Faulks a gunslinger, hip or otherwise? I thank God, and so should Mr Faulks, that he didn't get it; with a name like that, he'd have been catmeat within a week. The Clash had a roadie called Sebastian – Conran, some relation – and they treated him like we'd treated Onion Head. Two Sebastians and people would have tasted blood.

But of course I was noticed. I was the nearest thing they'd seen to a miracle since Iggy Pop walked on the hands of an audience one night – David Bowie also tried this and failed; the Man Who Fell To Earth, indeed – and let us not forget that this was the year 1976. The *NME*, which had been the feather-boa'd, eager-Biba'd belle of the bisexual ball during Glam found itself hungover and wearing too much of last night's make-up when the harsh light of Punk broke at last upon the suede-brained Seventies. They reached out, like drowning men, for the nearest possible lifebuoy. And, in doing so, put their arms around a pair of crocodiles who could shed no tears for them at all.

I heard I'd got the job a couple of months later, in the September of 1976, after a bit of to-ing and fro-ing and two interviews. My dad accompanied me to London from Bristol Temple Meads with all the sunny solemnity he had shown when taking me to the bal-let, sitting drinking his pint like he owned the place in a rough

Waterloo pub down the road from the massive IPC King's Reach Tower (where the *NME* was housed on the twenty-third floor, which it shared with *Horse and Hound* and *TitBits*) sitting drinking it in a shaft of sunlight right by the door so his darling, wicked, innocent daughter, despite everything, wouldn't have to put one sneakered foot inside such a sewer. When I think of him there that sunny day, delivering his daughter to something utterly alien to him, yet which he instinctively knew was probably her last chance to get a proper life, a life to be lived and not just processed, so cool and tall and Protestant, so utterly *calm*, I think of the Cranberries song. I know it's bad to think of a Cranberries song, but I can't help it; love makes Cranberries fans of us all. I think of that song where Dolores sings 'My father, my *father*, he liked me—' Coming out of that long dark night of adolescence, I could see again that he did.

Now, when there seemed to be a chance of *real* escape, not just a dream that could be crushed, my parents miraculously changed. This revealed to me, finally, the true beauty of them, and that there *was* no malice or desire to oppress me there – just fear. When I was put on the short-list of 200 after sending my mash note to Miss Smith, then of twenty after my first interview – with the long, louche, somewhat aristocratic deputy editor Tony Tyler, who took one look at my beautiful sixteen-year-old self in jeans and a white Boy Scout shirt, both tighter than a tourniquet, as I walked through his door, and said totally matter-of-factly, with the smut-free sex-talk that only a happily married man who's good in bed can pull off, 'You should know right now that if you get this job, every musician you meet will try to have sex with you. Even the queers, with that behind. It would be best for you in the long run if you told them very nicely that if they really want to fuck someone, they should go fuck themselves' – I began to float around the house in a very fatigued manner, saying that yes, it was all great fun but *not really* what I wanted from life. It was a bit . . . commercial. What about my . . . Art? The effect I was aiming for was sort of Virginia Woolf being offered the job of being Wolf on *Gladiators*. But naturally I didn't mean it. I was just being perverse. You know me.

But my mother didn't, of course. Well, I had spent the best part of the last four years deliberately making myself a stranger. While my father only ventured the amazing notion that he should *come in to the interview with me next time and explain my awkwardness to Nick Logan, the editor*! – can you *imagine* how such a snooty sixteen-year-old, well aware of the *NME*'s fast rep, took this? – my mother went berserk. 'Your chance!' she kept yelling, pointing at me, then at herself, then at me again. 'Your *chance*!' – banging her own collarbone with her fist.

I looked at her and saw how much, now escape was possible, she really did want me to be different. I was going away, but it had taken that to make me come home. For the first time in my life, I said those dread words every clever teenager must say, later if not sooner. Best just take a deep breath, and get it over with: 'I didn't mean it, Mum!'

I hadn't meant it, that I didn't want it. Why would someone not want their life, that they'd asked to be reserved for them a long time ago? I was just playing cool now, because it was so close and real.

Up I went again for the second interview, on the short-list of twenty. This time it was Nick Logan, the editor, who would ask the questions. The minute I stepped into his office I smelt trouble. I very much believe in the chemical theory of attraction, sexual or otherwise; I believe we choose even our most platonic friends by the way they smell. It's nothing to do with cleanliness or body odour; I've loved smelly people and loathed squeaky-clean ones. But the nose has it, definitely.

I had done so well in the first interview because, on some level, Tony Tyler smelled like my dad – calm, sexually confident, sexually *verboten*, kind; for want of a better word, *tall*. Nick Logan, God help him, probably smelled like me: skinny, rattled, scum-surfing. He stood up and shook my sweaty hand with his sweaty hand; he was no taller than me. He looked like someone half a year ahead of me at school, with cropped hair and an ACE T-shirt. Later, of course, I learned he had been a big Mod. They all looked like that in later life; scared stiff, because they'd glimpsed Nirvana and settled for Neasden. Or, in Logan's case, Wanstead.

We sat down.

'Someone's got the job,' Logan told me straight away, just to put me at my ease.

'Oh. Congratulations,' I said numbly. Fucking *sadist*.

'Yeah . . . a real young Turk . . . twenty-two . . . works in a gin distillery.' Logan's eyes gleamed like a loony's. He pulled himself together. 'Umm . . . Tony says I should see you. And Kate, Tony's girlfriend, she insisted.' Kate Phillips was a beautiful and clever writer at the *NME*, who had recently left in contempt at the Boys Club – or rather, Guys Club – office atmosphere and set herself up in a Sussex love nest with Tony T, which made total sense. Kate was also the daughter of the publisher of the *NME*, which was a bit of luck and quite prescient for me. I have always relied on the kindness of women.

'Kate read your review . . . we'd stopped reading them by then because there were so many –' *Cheers*, Nick! '– but Kate said it was only fair and she kept reading them and then yours came up.' He made it sound about as exciting and desirable as a hairball from a kitty.

'Oh.' Jeepers, I was speechless.

'So, umm . . . what groups do you like?'

'I like the Ramones,' I said carefully. I hoped I pronounced it right. Truth to tell, I was appalled by what I'd heard of Punk on after-dark Radio One – the Ramones and the Damned's 'New Rose'. I thought it was a bloody shambles. 'Call that singing?' – Punk instantly made me into a sixteen-year-old Colonel Blimp.

But hell, it was my lifeline. I wasn't about to wrap it around my neck and commit suicide, not now there was a real chance I might live.

'Yeah? I like the Ramones.' He seemed a bit more human now. I decided to shock him.

'But I like the Isley Brothers more.'

'Really?' He sat up straight. 'Do you like dance music?'

'I love it!' I leaned forward. 'I love George Macrae, Johnny Bristol, Eddie Kendricks—'

'Stax, Philadelphia, Invictus?'

'I love it! My favourite record is "Sweet Soul Music" by Arthur Conley.'

'"Sweet Soul Music"! But you're only sixteen!—' He seemed positively gleeful, twitching like a maniac.

'Old enough!' I leered.

I'd overstepped the mark. He remembered that he was Nick Logan, Ace Face overseer of the world's best-selling pop music magazine, hipper than a zipper and twice as hard. He was on a one-man mission to make the *NME the* Punk *Hansard* and he wasn't going to be fingered as no Northern soul-dancing fool.

He sat back in his chair. 'Someone's got the job, as I say. But we'll let you know.'

But I knew already; don't forget, it was *me* we were talking about. If one job was filled, then another would make itself free. I knew my product; I had spent sixteen years perfecting it.

So when I heard I'd got the job, or the other job, a belated birthday present for my seventeenth in the shape of a telegram delivered by a leather boy on a motor bike, the first time a telegram had been delivered in our street which spoke of a life rather than a death, I felt, strangely, for the first time in my sentient life, *relaxed*. At last I could be myself, because now Myself would be Somebody. I had literally made something out of nothing. This is how I wrote about that moment in my first novel *Ambition*: 'It was all so predictable somehow, her irresistible rise. She sat on the window-sill biting her thumbnail and looking out over the playground where her heart had been broken and her fate had been sealed, and she wished that somehow she could have been given some choice in the matter of her ambition and the success it would inevitably bring.'

Well, well, well; my mind stretched out like a cat in the sun. I felt like a julep, languid and long gone. *Well, well, well* – so this is how it feels to come home.

I was on my way to London and to fame – places I'd never been except in day-dreams and day trips – and it felt like going home. Speech, which had always felt like a shabby and badly mastered second language to me, could at last be abandoned as a bad job.

Because I was going to be a writer. I was going to speak my mother tongue.

Downstairs, I heard my mother crying.

And there it was, the train, swinging low round that bend and coming for to carry me home, to a place I'd only been to four times in my life. I hoisted my cheap suitcase. I felt terrified and free and more myself than I ever would again.

'Right. I'm off, then,' I said to my father, for all the world as if preparing to nip out for a can of Tizer and a brace of Bounty bars. I kissed him on the cheek and jumped aboard the London train. I felt light as the Slimcea girl; the world, previously such a weight upon my cold shoulders, now seemed like a Bouncy Castle under my feet.

My mother wouldn't come, as per; only he was hard enough to give away everything he had in the flesh. As I leaned photo-genically through the open window and reached out on reflex, with no idea of anything so weird as reciprocated physical affection, my father, my Bill, took my hand and looked at me with the full force of his endless, stubborn, perfect love. If I'd been a dog, he'd have kissed me.

'Be good,' he said.

And I was.

CHAPTER EIGHT

Young Guns, Having Some Fun

'That's your office,' someone said, pointing. Rudely.

I stumbled in, blind with terror. A boy in a white T-shirt was taping a photograph of James Dean to a glass partition above his desk. He turned round. 'Are you Julie Burchill?'

'Yes.'

'I'm Tony Parsons.'

He held out his hand. He was a boy of medium height and best described as 'fit', in both the wholesome and carnal senses of the word. He looked alarmingly three-dimensional in a way that I suddenly realised other people had not. He made others look like paper dressing-dolls. He had a fit hand on the end of a fit arm. I looked at it. Did he want me to bite it? I giggled. This punk protocol was going to be a pain, obviously.

He looked at me curiously, turned away casually, then turned back, picked me up and sat me high on top of a filing cabinet without drawing a breath.

I stared at him, amazed. Then we started laughing and didn't stop for years.

I liked Tony Parsons a whole lot. More than I'd liked anyone in my life. He was bellicose and self-dramatizing to a ridiculous extent – he made a bull in a china shop look like a Capodimonte shepherdess in a glass case – but hell, I'd probably have been like that if I'd have been a boy from our background, too. He was from new-town Essex; his dad was a war hero, his mum a dinner lady. He was, it must be said, *immaculately* working class, just like me. No room for doubt or insinuations of lower-middle wankiness *here*. We literally *smelled* each other's blood royal, like two toffs meeting in the jungle and changing into their dinner-jackets without consultation. One of us might have been cowed. Together, we were fearsome. I try now to imagine what we seemed like to the staff of the *NME*, and I can't. I just laugh. We must have seemed so *frightening*. We were, indeed, half mad. But all there. We just knew, which is unusual for both the working class and the music press, exactly *what was going on*. No wonder we went berserk.

I should never have married him (good God, no one should have married *either* of us!) but Tony was just *so* impressive. He impressed everyone. The staff of the *NME* pretended they weren't, at least for a while – Nick Kent was the only one with enough of his own spotlight to fall like a trembling leather leaf, at first glance. The punk bands, on the other hand, hung around him slack-jawed and starry-eyed; he was the boy who'd beat them up at school, but he was *smart*. Smarter than them. (Not difficult, admittedly, but still.) The Sex Pistols and the Clash, let alone the lessers, vied for his attention, for his eyes only; to the groupies and the record labels and their own managers they showed only contempt. But around Tony, they all did a passable imitation of the Red Sea with a major crush on Moses.

In those years I met lots of famous people. But I never wanted to be like any of them. Truth be told, and at last it must be, I only wanted to be like *him*. And I've amazed myself in writing that. But unless I'm a very good liar, I can only feel it to be the truth. I wanted to be like him: the Writer, whom everyone makes a blushing, hushing arch for. And when I felt I was enough like him to have what I wanted, I left him.

'Help me, help me, help me, oh Jesus!'

One week into a new career in a new town and I am already in serious shtup. Shtup City, in fact. I am the girl who ran away from home rather than tell her mother that she had reached the menarche. How in the name of God was I supposed to tell a total stranger that I wanted to use her bathroom in order to urinate?

'I am the son, I am the heir, of a shyness that is criminally vulgar.' Steven Morrissey will say it one fine day, one final day. For now I am stuck in the bathroom at Julie Webb's house, pretending to be sick, because I found it less embarrassing to ask for the bathroom as a vomitarium substitute than I did to ask for it as a urinal. Only after I had relieved myself silently and mimicked spewing loudly did it occur to me that I had announced my nausea *one bite* into the stuffed peppers which Julie Webb had served me so kindly. Oh Jesus, now she'll think her cooking made me sick! Oh God, *why was I born?* Obviously I'm going to make the same balls-up of life in the big city as I did in the small-prawn provinces.

Julie Webb is the listings editor of the *NME*, a short, straight, practical girl who has not been allowed to join the Boys Club and is therefore way beyond cool in a way that we can't yet identify. 'Get out of her chair!' she'll shout at Nick Kent when he sits in my seat that first day, when I come in from my sad first working lunch of a 99 ice-cream eaten furtively on Waterloo Bridge while my senior colleagues (even Mr Parsnip, as I spitefully call him to myself, envious of his ease, has been whisked out to a lavish lunch by no less than CBS, Nick Logan's mash elegies obviously having paved the way before him) enjoy sumptuous feasts in smoke-filled restaurants. I have Cadbury's Flake all down my white Boy Scout shirt and I ask myself for the nth time what sort of stupid sadist invented the crumbly treat. 'Here, I've got a great idea for a chocolate bar – you bite it and it goes all over your clothes and the carpet!'

Nick Kent slinks off with a bad grace, while giving me the fish-eye. He habitually looks like a six-foot-three-inch lizard, standing up on its two back legs and dressed head to toe in leather. He is one of those naturally weird-looking people who have decided at some point that it would be pathetic and pointless to try to pass as normal, and so have made themselves even weirder. He can literally stop traffic. And empty lifts. When he gets into the lift on the ground floor of King's Reach Tower, it empties as if by mustard gas or magic. He wears no underwear and his behind hangs out of his leather trousers. Not everyone is as cool about Master Nick's appearance as the indigenous Anglo society, I soon find out; the first week I'm there, he staggers in with his usual bent-kneed gait and blood running down his face.

'Some Rastafarians chased me down Westbourne Grove when I was leaving my girlfriend's house!' he complains bitterly. 'They called me a batty bum-claat and threw half a brick at my head!'

'Jah, mon!' tut-tuts Neil Spencer, the resident white Rasta deputy editor fondly. Well, as Rasta as you can be when you're as bald as Friar Tuck on top, have a grating Northamptonshire accent and quite resemble Bugs Bunny in the mush department. 'They was only trying to make friends!'

Which is more than Nick Kent wants to do with *me*, obviously, especially after Julie Webb throws him out of my chair. I don't give a toss, basically. He's a middle-class wanker and a junkie and a freak to boot; rumour has it that Keith Richard was once copiously sick on his jacket after a prolonged smack binge *and Kent never washed it again*. Later his cred will sink to an all-time low when he repeatedly brings an unknown, nineteen-year-old Paula Yates up to the office, because he and Richard Hell are allegedly sleeping with her.

'Come round to dinner,' says Julie Webb to me and Tony, taking pity when everyone else, the Boys Club, is still circling us, sniffing. She is a clever and competent little lady who appears to have found personal happiness far beyond the shifting sands of the music industry; for this her colleagues pretend pity and secrete envy. And now I have pretended to secrete something nasty in her S-bend just because I am such a stupid, shy *prannet*. Really, what was I like? It occurred to me, as I stood there in Julie Webb's bathroom, dry-throatedly mimicking a grand finale to my phantom vomiting, that my parents and school-mates actually might have had a *point*. Maybe I *was* unbearable.

But really, so what? As luck would have it, the Unbearable Look was the New Look. It was bliss to be young in the second half of

1976 – when pop music finally lost its mind and came to its senses again, gloriously deflated and gorgeously defaced – but to be young and working at the *NME* was like dying and going to heaven, except you were around to write about it every week. *Of course* I was paralysingly shy, but snakebite and speed gave me front. I was very quickly notorious and, within a month of setting pen to paper, anyone who was any fun on the scene knew who I was. 'So *you're* the famous Julie Burchill!' said Paul Weller. When Johnny Rotten sat at my feet one night and began to talk at me, I had his number. His big put-down, I knew, was 'You're too old'. So I interrupted him: 'How *old* are you?'

'What? Me? . . . I'm *nineteen*,' he stuttered, stunned.

'Oh, you're too *old*.' I sneered. It was a Rock Dream come true. You could stuff the Algonquin and the dry Martinis the way you could stuff the olives; make mine a line and a lager dahn the Roxy, John.

The *NME* staff were generally very nice to me to start with, even if Tony and I *had* put their coke-ridden noses out of joint a little – especially the Class of Seventy-three *enfants terribles* (translation: pain in the ass under forty) who had been flavour of the month before punk came along and rendered their Afros, boas, satin 'n' tat somewhat redundant. They did tend to call one 'Man', which grates if you're a girlie, and one's working-class credentials did tend to make them a little *chippy*. 'Stop flexing your roots, Man!' one of them said to me when I innocently cracked open a tasty tin of Tizer one day.

They were lower middle class and middle class from the Home Sweet Home Counties, and they hadn't observed many flaming prole youths at close quarters – and then only from the wrong side of a Doc Marten boot, most likely. We were like unicorns to them, mythical beasts – the exotic, wondrous stuff of legend, but probably not real. And imagine your shock when, upon meeting one of these creatures, it's *not* nuzzling up to you with big adoring Bambi eyes – gee whizz, you handsome hippie hunk, you! – like in the Rackham drawings, but trying to run you through with its horn! You can go off people, you know.

Of course I never intended to run them through with my horn, or even with the quite sizeable black-and-silver switchblade which Tony Parsons brought me swiftly back from Dunkirk after his first foreign jaunt – 'So you can defend yourself, Angel!' Their fear was nothing but a by-product of my own cultivation of Attitude – copyright 1976, before Attitude as we know it existed – which I realised within a couple of weeks of working there was going to be as essential as an oxygen mask to one as deeply bashful as myself; it was either that or bail out to the cardboard box factory on the midnight train to Bristol.

At first, it must be said, I was very scared of the *NME* staff, who seemed to me tremendously old – they ranged from about twenty-five to forty – and worldly. But after a while, I understood that – like the spiders and snakes of legend, according to my parents, let alone my gran's vicious budgerigar Billy – *they were more scared of me than I was of them.* And to deflect my own terrors, I began to play on theirs; cleaning my nails with my shiv and leaning in their doorways, sneering at them bug-eyed as they sweet-talked A&R men on the phone, snorting speed off their desks while they were trying to work (and offering them a line, too, which was meant to be *extra* bad, as the self-dramatising old queens were always going *cold turkey*, gobble gobble!, as though it wasn't just *speed* but some really major morphine'n'laudanum cocktail they'd been quaffing) – just a little something to whiten Mother's Afro, really.

You see, we hadn't even started yet – *that* was the Kinder-Surprise we had up our slashed cap sleeves for the old darlings, did they but know it! Next came our most daring creation – apart from ourselves – yet: the KinderBunker, named by Neil Spencer in a periodic fit of disapproval. 'Man, them white powders gwan make you slow!' Jah Spence would warn, his reefer-addled brain barely able to put even such a dinky little sentence together. Whenever we played our Clash and Sex Pistols white labels he would rouse himself from his drug-fugged stupor long enough to mimic the performance of a mad pogo stick all through the not so much open-plan as ajar-plan offices – we were each given our own little compounds for two, but the partitions didn't reach to the ceiling and there were no doors.

We'd see about that, T and me leered as we watched Jah Spence pogo all the way out to the secretaries' compound, frightening the gently raised Fiona, Margaret and Val quite badly. The door jambs may have been empty, but two lively minds with more dash than cash soon tumbled that they could be lined with barbed wire and have attractive multicoloured plastic stripping hung from their tops. The barbed-wire motif was cheap and cheerful, and easily continued along the top of the partitions; broken glass made a shiny, optimistic contrast when alternated with it. Finally, a charming noose, hung high slap-bang in the middle of the room, provided an interesting conversation piece. Which would usually start when, on arrival, the charming young proud householders Julie and Tony would find that *yet another smelly hippie* had tried to dismantle it – no doubt fearing that its negative noosey vibes would sour the beatific atmosphere of the place – and demand loudly of the lurking company '*Who's been fucking with my noose?*' A bit like *Goldilocks and the Three Bears*, only not. 'The KinderBunker was worth a couple of thousand a year in itself,' wrote Peter York in *Style Wars*. So it just shows how you can achieve the de luxe look on a tight budget.

And as for beatific – what a bloody scream! The first day there, T and I were shocked to hear the otherwise decent-seeming Julie Webb introduce two long-haired thirty-somethings in the next compound with the words: 'Tony and Julie, this is Steve and Phil.' Then, *sotto voce* but deadly serious: 'They're the office scapegoats. If anything goes wrong, just say it was their fault and Logan won't take it any further.'

No kidding, I thought, eyeing the inelegant modern phone on my new desk thoughtfully. I had at that time a morbid fear of talking on the telephone, probably due in some part to my piping voice which, though remarkable to the point of risibility in one-on-one contact, rose to the heights of Boop-Bott burlesque when transported through the evil medium of the telephone wires. 'Is your mother in?' salesmen still ask me on the phone.

'Probably,' I reply, 'but I couldn't swear to it. Why don't you ring her and ask her? BECAUSE I AM A THIRTY-SEVEN-YEAR-OLD WOMAN WHO HASN'T LIVED WITH HER MOTHER FOR TWENTY YEARS, THANKYOUVERY-MUCH!'

A fiendish plan came to me there and then: to rip my phone out of the wall, fray the wires and claim I hadn't done it myself. That way I wouldn't be forced to make calls for a few days, at least. In my crazy little padded-cell playpen of a brain it didn't occur to me that I'd be told to use Tony's instead. So I did – and, of course, I was. But a couple of scapegoats right next door, eh? Cosy.

Not that Logan was a man much inclined to take issue about anything, I soon found out. Though already well on the way to becoming one of the most innovative editors ever, whose maga-zines *The Face* and *Arena* would not just lead but create whole new magazine markets, he wasn't what you'd call hands-on at this point. In fact, the only things he ever seemed to put his hands on were the cans of spray-paint which he used to lock himself into his office with – Tony called it 'the West Wing' – and spend his day spraying potential new logos on to huge pieces of cardboard. Sometimes, when we'd finished our 'ippie-tormenting duties for the day and were feeling very wicked, we'd go down to Logan's office and press our faces against the glass panel – Tony's face above, mine below – and just leave them there, grotesquely squashed, until he finally looked up and saw us. He'd shriek most satisfactorily and run over to pull down the blind that could cover the glass panel.

Logan liked Tony, but he didn't like me. He had his reasons. I was pretty awful – totally belligerent in the office, totally pathetic out of it – and I wasn't exactly out there getting the scoops. I had been dropping heavy hints about my fantasy Sapphism and one day Logan said in an editorial meeting when I wasn't there, 'The only thing that would interest that girl is if she found out Elvis was gay.' He had a point. Truth to tell, I wasn't gone a whole bundle on punk now that I was hearing it twenty-four hours a day – it was even worse than I'd expected! But Logan thought I loved it, so to punish me he started having me sent to interview hippies and headbangers, usually at some unearthly hour of the morning.

I trotted gamely on, keeping my head clean and my nose down, until I was caught slipping a teaspoonful of speed into Country Joe McDonald's English breakfast tea. It made perfect sense to me; as I knew by now, speed opened people up like fast-mo flowers and made them talk a blue streak. As I knew nothing about Mr McDonald and had been instructed to get a few thousand words out of it, what could be better than to slip him the treat you can eat between meals in his cuppa? Wouldn't you know it, a snoopy PR person from his poxy record company saw me doing it while old Joe was in the can and when he came back she went into her *J'accuse* number. Mr McDonald was quite sweet about it, but wouldn't you just *know* he'd had loads of hippie friends die of drug overdoses in the Sixties and Seventies – including old Janis Joplin, whom he'd been in love with, amazingly, which just shows you that people who don't take drugs can be really weird too – and was very, very anti-drugs indeed. I took my ticking-off like a man – that is, with lots of pouting and sulking – and arrived back at the office thinking to hear no more of the incident.

Was I wrong. In this little local moral panic, Logan saw the perfect springboard he had been waiting for in order to jump up and down going boing-boing-boing, incandescent as Zebedee in his anger, before plunging head first into the whitewater ride of his own irritation. Did I *realise* what I was doing? This was my *big* chance. My *only* chance. Did I *want* to go back to the biscuit factory in Bristol?

'Box factory,' I said sullenly. 'My mother makes cardboard boxes.'

'Unlike you, who only make trouble!' Old Nick had had enough, it seemed. 'Get out of my office, Julie. I don't want to see you for a while. And neither,' he finished spitefully, 'will any record company or any artist, once they find out what you've been up to.'

As I went through the door I had to hang my head, supposedly in shame, but really to hide my smile. I might have only been in the music business five minutes, but really – become a pariah, an outcast, would I, for slipping someone drugs on the sly? I doubted it, somehow!

'You OK, Angel?' Tony asked me sympathetically as I slouched back into the Bunker.

'Not really. The 'ippie's PR bird only blabbed to Logan, didn't she?'

'Jeez!' Tony's fist crashed down upon his desk. '*Bloody* 'ippies!'

Bloody 'ippies, indeed. But they probably did me a big favour, despite themselves. They thought I was a punk and sure enough I became one; a self-fulfilling prophecy which confirmed their worst nightmares. Because, basically, they were hippies and so they thought we wanted to kill them.

We didn't, of course. We just wanted to have a bit of fun at their expense. And they deserved it. For years they'd been eulogising rawness and proleness, the psychosis and the violence of rock-'n'roll. Now here it was, standing sneering in front of them, and they couldn't stomach it. *We* were the people, it was to turn out, whom their parents had warned them about; they were cruising for a bruising and we obliged them, like the obedient little proles we were.

There were punks and bloody 'ippies, then, and never the twain should meet. But I had not reckoned on how the heart behaves. The wild black heart, especially.

CHAPTER NINE

Sleeping with the NME

Talk about hippies; there were a right pair in the compound directly next door to us. The real McCoy, I mean; been there, smoked that, had the police caution. The other people in the office were Hippy Lite; they smoked dope on high days and holidays, and their hair probably wouldn't pass muster in a Territorial Army passing-out parade. They knew someone who'd been in a protest march, once. But you could be positive that when the final spliff had been rolled and the final Rizla binned, they'd be voting Lib-Dem in Putney with the best, or the worst, of them. There came a point in the Seventies where the 'hippie' look became the conformist look and you saw many a member of the National Front sporting longish hair and sloppy T-shirts. In the famous 1977 National Front–SWP run-in at Lewisham, we knew our side because *we* had the short hair.

Not so the Heads Next Door. Charles Shaar Murray and Mick Farren, though young by my standards now – needless to say, they seemed ready for a bus pass at the time – were, in their late twenties and mid-thirties respectively, genuine veterans of the hippie wars; *Schoolkids Oz*, *International Times*, love-ins, be-ins, you name it. And Tony and I, in the best tradition of next-door neighbours, liked to torment them a good deal, I'm afraid.

Do you know what an Isro is? It's an Afro, but Jews wear it.

Charlie and Mickey, as we were encouraged to call them – they were genuinely nice fellows – were both Jewish and boasted fine Isros, as well as full-on leather jackets to show that they weren't *really* smelly 'ippies who could be pushed around, but basically as 'ard as the rest of us. We had to titter. And we had to, just had to, because we were young and dumb and it was irresistible, buy packets of cigarillos, smoke them to the stub, climb up on to Tony's desk next to the partition and flick the burning butts over into next door's. One point for getting a burning butt on to the carpet and making it smoulder, five for a desk-top, TEN POINTS FOR GETTING THE HIPPIE IN THE HAIR, HEH HEH HEH! LOOK OUT, HIPPIE ON FIRE! If we were lucky enough to get them in the Isro we'd then rush into their office: 'Charlie, Mickey, there's a fire!' we'd plead, clutching each other.

'God . . . where, Man?' they'd say, stumbling up, stoned again, from their seats.

'*There*!' We'd point at their heads and run away, hysterical with laughter.

Nevertheless, they kept on being nice to us. Charlie was so decent that he took me out of the YWCA, which was admittedly a bit surreal when you had to go home there after seeing the Sex Pistols on the Screen on the Green, and back to live with himself and his wife, Susan, in a tenement at the Angel. This really was the sleazy, glamorous heart of the city and I knew I'd finally arrived.

Susan Murray was a tall, long-haired blonde girl in her mid-twenties, with an hour-glass figure and really big breasts. Yes, and I *know* what you're thinking – it does look good on paper, doesn't it? She was dead intelligent, too. But she was intelligent in a bad way, a wasteful, middle-class, unfocused way which means that you *think* about things so much that you just end up sitting there *stewing*, like an old pot of tea, and then all your brains go bitter in your head until they make you stupid, not smart. Truly, the over-examined life ends up not worth living. She didn't work, just slept all day, then Charlie would come home from the office at night to his joint and his line of amphetamine sulphate all laid out, like a parody of pipe and slippers.

He'd tell her stories from the office. 'Tell me about the New Girl,' she'd say. I was apparently the topic of much conversation at Murray Towers. I was always doing something naughty. Dosing country crooners with speed. Announcing in an editorial meeting that I was a *lesbian*, and what did they think of *that*? Acting thoroughly self-righteously, but righteously so, whenever dwarves were sent to the *NME* offices by some scummy record company to promote a record that invariably had *nothing* to do with dwarves – they were just a cheap gimmick. Whenever I heard the assembled staff tittering stonedly after lunch in the lobby, my ears would go up; 'Dwarf Alert!' I'd think. And I'd stomp out, push through the titters, tell the dwarves 'Please! Go home now!' and take revenge on the onlookers by going into their compounds and kicking their wastepaper baskets over. Well, I was only just seventeen.

So we'd all three of us at Murray Towers do amp sulph all night long, playing records that we couldn't ever leave on for more than ninety seconds, then Charlie and I would drag ourselves to King's Reach Tower after three hours' sleep or so. I was seventeen, Charlie all of twenty-seven, but we must have resembled veterans of some dreadful battle as we lurched on and off Tube trains on our way to work each morning. 'Not long, now, C. I've got you.' 'Wake up, Jools. We're at Blackfriars. Tell you what, make it up the escalator and you can have a sit-down at the Embankment.' And to think that eight weeks before I'd been suffering through Double Maths as only the truly short-sighted can suffer. I certainly had come a long way, baby.

I was starting to enjoy being at the *NME* office. As luck would have it, my sugar-substitute attempts to prise a blue streak of chatter out of Joe McDonald had resulted in Logan handing down the decree to his deputy, Jah Spence, and all the commissioning editors, that I was *not allowed* to interview *anyone*. I was still pretty shy, so he was doing me a favour. Instead I was dispatched to Soho each morning to pick up all the strange special-interest import magazines I could find, as well as staple stuff like the *National Enquirer*, *Circus* and Rona Barrett's *Hollywood Reporter*. Then I'd

lug them back to the office and sit with my feet up on the desk
reading them until I found an interesting snippet which might be
made into a stylised little story for the opening section, 'Thrills'.
This was lots of fun. I wrote about showbiz divorces and the very
first Pet Rock. It certainly didn't *feel* like work. I thought about my
Hard Girl enemies, slogging out their guts and losing their looks in
some factory or grease shop, and I couldn't help but laugh.

'Tell us the joke, sweetheart!'

Oh no, it was that man again! Mick Farren, the hippie next door,
supposed embodiment of all I, a newly minted punk icon, hated,
walked into my compound and my heart fractured. Or my crotch.
Something, anything. I gaped at him. I felt that I was being set up
to play the lead in an awful, purple punk-hippie version of *Romeo
and Juliet*, and I couldn't even remember my opening lines.

He took out his Sinex spray and applied it copiously to his big,
bruised nose. 'Come over tonight.' You bet! 'Meet Ingrid, my old
lady, at last. You'll like her.' Won't, don't, can't, *shan't*!

On paper, Charlie and Mickey were two middle-class Jewish
men in early middle age who had been through the Alternative
Sixties trip in a major way. On all fours, they couldn't have been
more different. Charlie was obviously a mummy's boy, plump,
pink and petulant. But Mickey seemed both dangerous and attractive because he appeared genuinely to despair of life while never,
ever whining about it – in my book, which is this one, whining self-
pity in a man is to sex what a bucket of cold water is to a pair of
fornicating dogs. On the contrary, he had thrown himself into the
commercial mainstream with great zeal, as had many of his
Underground *compadres* and, with all the sour energy of the
thwarted idealist, had a finger in a score of quick-fix pies, be they
fast books or short stories for soft-core porn magazines.

But he just *looked* so disillusioned; his big, battered face seemed
absolutely beautiful to me and he had totally let himself go. He was
slumping willingly into old age, it appeared to me, because youth
hadn't brought him anything worth having; to him, changing the
world. From now on, it would take all the drugs and sex and cash
in that rotten world to tie a tourniquet around that big, bleeding

heart. I really, really admired the way he abused his big old burned-out body and I wanted to be the same. It looked like the nearest you could get to staying a working man in the mimsy media playpen – hurting yourself, in the pursuit of pleasure. That was what *we* did.

He had been a White Panther, whatever that was, and you could hear him on an MC5 record, inciting the audience. He wrote every week to Wayne Kramer in jail, and in interviews Wayne Kramer referred to Mickey as 'my brother'. And he walked – ooo, he walked like the John Wayne of Ladbroke Grove. Like he was *sore*. When someone told me that as well as being a radical hero he was a sexual sadist there was no stopping me. Well, *obviously*. Like I say, I was *seventeen* and it was the Seventies. We were well stupid back then.

'That Mick Farren!' I complained to Mrs Murray when we were lying in her bed one afternoon. Of course, like all those in love, I used any excuse, even negative ones, to mention his name. 'Apparently he said to Charlie "Don't let Julie move in with you, man. She'll get off with your wife."'

Susan laughed in delight and kissed me. 'Which you have!'

'What?' I was outraged. 'We've never had *sex*!'

'*That* isn't what "getting off" means, darling.' She smiled. 'Getting off can be this.' She touched my breast. 'Or this.' She kissed my mouth.

'Whaaat? . . . you're *joking*.' I thought about it. 'Boy . . . *really*. You learn something new every day.' I kissed her back, for a long time.

I understand that men are supposed to 'chase' women. I've never seen it that way. Any man who's presumptuous enough to chase a woman, *après* feminism and during stalking – stalkers, those goon-squad foot soldiers of the modern sex war – is a man who's not worthy of the name. It's just rude. On the other hand, I wouldn't give the time of day to a man who played hard to get, either – that's dead naff, like a Babs Cartland heroine. No, what a man is meant to do is stand about looking sexy until a woman decides she'll have sex with him. Then he's got to make her come three times before he does. To me, that's the birds and the bees – that's the basics. And any man who says otherwise probably isn't sexually attractive; and any woman who says otherwise probably can't come.

I'd worked this out by now, at seventeen. I'd lost my technical virginity – to Tony Parsons, Lord help me; more of *this* tale of woe later – and I'd lost my *real* virginity, several weeks later, to a nineteen-year-old blond-haired boy who was still at Cambridge. Losing your *real* virginity is when you first *come* with someone, I believe. A bit like the Queen having two birthdays. So I knew the score. I may have been too young to vote and two steps removed from virginity, he may have had one foot in the grave and have fucked himself stupid – literally – but I knew the way things were meant to be. I took to strolling into his office after downing half a shandy of Dutch courage every afternoon and staring moodily at him, leaning in his doorway. He would look back at me, at first unbelieving, then fearful, finally resigned. He would spread his hands and shrug, gorgeously Hebraic, and I would go and sit on his desk and put my long slender feet in his lap. *Shut up* with the sick-bag there! You've got to remember what I looked like then, and how strange and sensual this thing was, while sulphed-out sexless punk raged all around us.

We were workmates; it was easy to keep manoeuvring us into taxis together. We were always heading for the same show at night. 'I've just remembered!' I'd gasp audaciously at Tony, pushing Charlie towards him. 'You go ahead – I'll go with Mickey.' Truth to tell, everyone was so stoned, speeding, sloshed out of their boxes at that time that this ruse never needed back-up.

Then it was bliss. I'd pour my darling mixed-up Mickey into a taxi, and sit and stare soulfully at him. He'd use his Sinex and mumble a bit, then he'd address me, always respectfully, with a strange declaration: 'You will die alone. Like Virginia Woolf,' or 'There are two kinds of women. Sisters – and pussy. And then there's you. Which makes *three* kinds of women.'

This was all well and good. It was nice to know that the one I adored respected me. But there comes a time when we're only flesh and blood, if you get my drift. Have you ever heard of that film title *Kiss Me, My Fool?* Then you'll know how I felt. Really!

'Drive on, driver.' I became used to saying this during the illicit dates that Mickey and I shared, usually because he'd passed out from drink. He had Ingrid waiting at home, I had Tony – who *wasn't* my boyfriend, but on the other hand lived just up the hall and for some reason would have felt perfectly within his rights to behead anyone I brought home, even a stray mongrel dog, on the grounds that they were coming between himself and his unhealthy obsession with me.

So that was my first great London love: driving around our capital in a black taxi, with the burnt-out brain of my beloved in my lap. After an hour or so he'd sober up and say, 'I'm not – I'm not—' and I'd reluctantly take him home to Notting Hill and drop him off to the legal tender mercies of his Ingrid. I'm not, I'm not – what? Yours? Guilty? In love? Search me, guv. I rode home, seventeen, perfect, crying, lost, incandescent with life. Things would never be so full-on, low-down, fucked-up great again.

In the Seventies there were a lot of toothy Mormon morons hanging around the pop charts tormenting us with covers of Fifties high-school letter-sweater drivel like 'Puppy Love' and 'Young Love, First Love' and 'The Twelfth of Never'. In such songs, teen romance is inevitably painted as something straightforward and simple, albeit heart-breaking. He loves you and you love him and if only it weren't for your bloody parents sticking their ruddy oar in, you'd be set up in the Little House on the Prairie with a coolerator of ginger ale and a juke box full of O'Jays records.

Wrong! In my experience, teenage sex, not to mention love, is one of the weirdest, most complicated and labyrinthine experiences known to man. You lost your Big V to X but you first came with Z. You're still in love with your best friend from school in a really *spiritual* sort of way, yet you dream of having it slipped to you from behind in a public lavatory by Y, an Older Man. Maybe we could have blamed it on the early influence of the gender-shocked David Bowie, insisting that 'Everyone's bisexual,

Man'. I do not know. But it certainly wasn't the home life of our own dear Gidget, from where I was standing.

You had to add to this – Tony playing guard dog down the hall, Mickey playing possum, Mrs Murray playing away at home, so to speak, Cambridge Blond playing havoc with my hormones every time he was down from Jesus (very suitably, as the air was thick with the name of his alma mater every time he lowered himself to get horizontal with me: 'Jesus!' 'Christ!' 'Oh, God!'; I was either having extremely good sex, or considering Theology as a future educational option) – the fact that I had found myself my very own stalker. As suited my perverse, not to say perverted nature, she was a teenage girl and her name was Jane Suck.

You must know, even if you're spectacularly dense, the way the words 'teenage girl' and 'sexy' go hand in hand in our language and our culture, if it can be called that. Well, if you're an ugly – not just a plain, but an ugly – teenage girl in that culture, your life is, I believe, a walking, talking, crying, dying living hell. Unless you're very intellectual or gifted or tough, I certainly wouldn't want to walk a mile in your Start-Rites.

What most ugly teenage girls learn to do, from a very early age, is play dead. Like someone who has been attacked and assaulted to the point of death will, when only pretending to be dead already can possibly stop the attacker from finishing you off. They stay quiet, they stand still and they try to blend into the background. Which, considering their complexions and the popularity of pebbledash in Bristol, was easier round our way than most, I suppose.

Jane Suck was no such blushing flower. Though goodness knows that she had had every chance a young girl can be given to embrace a living death. For a start, Jane came from Weston-super-Mare. This sleepy seaside town, some twenty minutes by train from Bristol, was the second home, during summer, of the local youth, a shimmering sunlit ritual which even Unpopulars and Weirdos participated in almost daily, going down and coming back on the local train through Keynsham and Nailsea and Yatton and Worle and Weston Milton, our check shirts knotted beneath our excuses for breasts and our spirits even higher, though we ceaselessly disparaged it as 'Weston-super-Mud' and it's *true*, you never did see the sea or, as we later found out, the sodding *Bristol Channel!* In the summer of 1996, both my marriages and my paparazzi-ridden great lesbian escape behind me, reconciled with my parents, I took my ten-year-old to the scene of my childhood frolics and, wearing diamonds bigger than my love bites, I rode with him along the sea-front and back in the rackety land train and anointed myself while moving at wrists and throats with Joy, the world's costliest perfume. Our friends the Americans were, as always, wrong; not only *can* you go home again, but to go home in style is the greatest revenge of all.

But love it though we did, during those eternal shiny early Seventies daytrips when the unions were stronger and the summers were longer, no one could ever accuse Weston of not being a backwater. It spawned – in every sense of the word – two famous citizens, Jeffrey Archer and John Cleese, who positively *bristle* with not being from Bristol, even, with being condemned by birth to treading water in some backwater for the rest of their unnaturals. If Jane had been a coward it would have been as easy a place as any in which to measure out your life in plastic Wall's ice-cream spoons.

Or maybe not. Maybe Jane would have stuck out – I just wrote 'struck out', accidentally I hope, and had to change it – anywhere, and *especially* in such a doily-centred environment as Weston. For Jane's fate, and face, were blighted by the most virulent case of acne I have ever seen in my life. You've heard the old joke about most men's ideal woman being one who goes all night long and then turns into a pizza? Jane looked like exactly that; that she had gone all night and now she was turning into said Italian savoury, starting with her face. Add this to a shaven head, sawn-off-at-knees stature and the sort of bulk that made her look as though she was wearing a Puffa jacket 24:7:52 and believe me, it was no one's idea. Least of all mine, whose ideal of female beauty has been, is and forever will be five foot eleven, size 10, silky-haired, smooth-skinned, green-eyed, cat-faced and answering to the name of Charlotte. No wonder I only get to sleep with a girl once every ten years.

But out there, in Weston, Jane had read my adolescent ramblings; been teased by my Sapphic posturing. And boy, did she like what she read. She chucked in her education – she was eighteen, a year older than me – and came to London, to be the next Julie Burchill. The next Julie Burchill! – the new Julie Burchill! – I've been hearing *that* one since I was seventeen and you know what? Damn me if I *still* haven't seen a one of them. New Julie Burchills are like Abominable Snowmen: sightings are quite often reported, but verification is ever elusive.

Anyway, *Sounds*, which was a music paper quite like the *NME* only crap, decided they wanted one just like me. And Jane was there, on their doorstep, teenage, alienated and boasting a stupid, sexually provocative name to boot. (This was another example of her special sort of bravery; people expect a girl called Suck to be one hot porno babe.) Of course they grabbed her – the first time she'd been grabbed *ever*, I bet.

See that? It's Onion Head all over again, isn't it? Pretty girls, no matter how hard they try, unless they're urban saints like Bambi, always end up tormenting ugly ones. But Jane didn't mind. She doted on me, phoned me at the office, was invited up – the fact that she was from Weston was the decider – was treated with a modicum of interest and then, right on cue, began to fall quite horribly in love with me. It ended, of course, where even a gentleman carrying a white stick, wearing dark glasses and being led by a Golden Labrador could have told me it would, while I, being seventeen and immortal, would not, of course, have believed him: me wearing a red kimono, the door of one mouldy room in Crouch End double-locked and Jane wielding a butcher's knife, hallucinating on crystal meth and demanding that I masturbate openly in front of her or else she'd slice me so far down the middle that I'd be able to bring myself off orally.

Happy days!

I remember my seventeenth year, and *only* my seventeenth year actually, as a maelstrom of sexual intrigue. While Jane was pursuing me, I was stalking Mickey; drunken old fool that he was, he didn't get the hint for ages. I soon realised that I would have to take affirmative action; nothing tacky or obvious, *obviously*, just a discreet little nudge in the right direction, i.e. bed. So I poured myself into my Levis, sprayed my upper torso with what looked from a distance like a white cap-sleeved T-shirt and through which you could easily calculate my age in years by the detail around my nipples, shrugged on my leather jacket with a sang-froid that only a seventeen-year-old can pull off, stole a red, red apple from a greengrocer's in Westbourne Grove and turned up on his doorstep one morning when I knew his girlfriend was away.

It was high noon but when he opened the door I knew he had just woken up. His Isro appeared to have exploded. He rubbed his bloodshot eyes with beautiful fists. 'Julie?'

'Hello, Mickey.' I bit into the apple. He gulped and swallowed. (See? We were already as one. BUT NOT AS MUCH AS WE SOON WOULD BE, HEH HEH HEH!) 'The same.' I smouldered up his three doorsteps at him. 'Aren't you going to ask me . . . in?' It's weird, ever since I became sexually aware I seem to have thought, spoken and acted like someone straight out of a *Carry On* film.

'Yeah . . . sure.' He stepped back, as he always did for me, and I passed him into the hallway. He pointed up. 'The flat's up there.'

'Right.' I put my hand on the bannister and felt him tremble. 'Mickey?'

'Yeah?'

'You know this thing sado-masochism?'

'Yeah . . .'

'Can you show me, please?'

He did.

CHAPTER TEN

Punk Rock –
My Part in its Downfall

When it comes to sex, I find that a quite alarming number of people, mostly men, seem to have a sort of selective amnesia. When *they* were young bloods, they didn't care *where* they put it. Cousin, friend's mother, friend's sister – best friend's girl, or preferably fiancée, is always a timeless sexual-treachery classic popular with men from all walks of life, I have generally found.

But once *they've* decided to make like a stomach taking Alka Seltzer and settle, when *they've* got their whip and slippers under the bed of the sugar snack of their choice, what happens? B.A.V.s – Born Again Virgins! It's a sumptuous hypocrisy on a par only with America's attitude to revolutions. You know – well, yes, *we* had one but we were *allowed* to because it was about *freedom*. But you – Nicaragua/El Salvador/Cuba – *you're* not allowed to have one because then, then it's about *Communism*! So *there*!

Men are like that. Both my husbands were *very* free with themselves before they married me and, as with most men, the fruit they could see hanging on the tree in their next-door neighbour's garden was inevitably the juiciest looking. In the case of one of the characters with whom I committed altar-saunter, I was of course already married to the first one when we began our affair. But the moment I flirted mildly with one of his friends, or come to that ran off with a pussycat, he just couldn't see either the comparison or his own post-dated culpability and thus felt it to be his total right to paint me as the villain of the piece. Men!

Anyway, back to the narrative. Tony, for some reason – selective sexual amnesia, most likely – seemed to have forgotten somehow that we had only had one nasty, brutish and short (though not short enough in my book) shag, to which I had responded with mild dismay, as though someone had trodden heavily on my toe. In truth, that was what it felt like to me; a cross between that and having a tooth pulled without benefit of anaesthetic. But for some weird reason Tony seemed to think I was his *girlfriend*.

I don't know what the usual reaction to his performance was, but in the days which followed the non-event my deflowerer didn't seem best pleased with my inability distinctly to detect a terra-firma-shifting situation after a few paltry pokes with his perfectly ordinary pride and joy. During a lunch-time repast in our Waterloo local, the Rose and Crown (which might better have been named the Nose and Clown, considering its proximity to and patronage by the louche, foolish folk at the *NME*), he leaned across the table and said in a quiet, mean voice: 'Has it ever occurred to you that you're a lesbian?'

I may have been young and raw, but I knew immediately what an incredibly naff thing this was to say. To *me*, especially! I mean, it may not have been the truth, but I'd been shouting my Sapphism from the roof-tops ever since day one in the capital. Mine wasn't the love that dare not speak its name, it was the bloody love that wouldn't shut up! Even if I hadn't ever *done* anything! It was a *teen* Thang! So I just sat there, looking at him. But he wouldn't be told.

'Has it ever occurred to you that you're frigid?'

Oh, really! I'd heard that that was popular among boys who'd received a less than rapturous reception in the sackeroo, but I really couldn't believe that I was *hearing* it now. So I sat, still looking him straight in the eye, and I changed my face. I didn't smile – nothing so crass. I just changed my face so it was in the queue for wry, moving up slowly but surely on the inside all the time. And he backed off, as bullies tend to do when you look them in the eye and silently say IF YOU TAKE ONE STEP FURTHER, I

PERSONALLY WILL TELL YOU SOMETHING WHICH
YOU KNOW ABOUT YOURSELF BUT HAVE NEVER PUT
INTO WORDS AND WHICH WILL CAUSE SERIOUS,
PERHAPS FATAL DAMAGE TO YOUR SELF-IMAGE. I
may not be able to speak any foreign languages, but I'm really good
at saying quite subtle and complicated things with my big green
eyes.

Besides – a frigid lesbian, *moi*? Hardly! When Big Brother
wasn't around, it was rum, sodomy and the lash all the way.
Luckily he kept being sent off on tour with stupid bands, so I had
loads of time to develop my repertoire.

It was weird to be having one's formative sexual experiences
against the backdrop of punk rock; if music really were the food of
love, I'd have been pure as the driven snow. The more I heard of
it, the more I hated it; I used to go back to my lowly room after
another ear-bleeding night dahn the Roxy and soothe my soul with
the sweet sounds of the Isley Brothers, playing 'Live It Up' and
'Summer Breeze' until even Tony shouted down the hall for me to
'pack it in now, Angel! It's four in the morning!'

Did I fancy any of the bands? No, not really. If you knew them
even slightly, as I did, you didn't really fancy them at all because
their personal habits were so disgusting. They were all spit and
snot and stains and smells, especially the Sex Pistols. The only
exceptions were Paul Simenon of the Clash, who was just beautiful and easily as adorable as he was lovely, and Joe Strummer.
Frankly, I adored Joe. But he had twelve girlfriends and he was
faithful to all of them, in his fashion, so that was that. I also had the
most massive crush on Chrissie Hynde and used to follow her
around like a puppy. She would wear a condom safety-pinned to
her lapel – this was *years* before condoms became common currency. Finally she noticed me and we became friends. But she still
scared me to death. I could feel myself flinch when she touched
me. Once she sang the Rolling Stones song 'Under My Thumb' to
me, alone in a room, and I literally swooned and thought I was
going to die. She was the most charismatic and enchanting woman
I'd ever met; Cleopatra meets John Wayne. If I'd been an animal,

she might have treated me better. (My dad and Prince all over again, obviously.)

London may have been once more the curiosity-shop window of the Western world and punk might be making it on to the covers of *Time* and *Newsweek*, but this was hardly Swinging London Mark Two. Far from being bright and beautiful young things whose cup ran over, Sixties-style, with sex, cash and confidence, we punks were what we looked: a miserable, suspicious, querulous lot, perpetually expecting someone to come along and tell us that, heh heh, it had all been one big *prank* and we really *hadn't* been given contracts by the *NME* and EMI. Back to the dole, thou cream-faced prole!

And so we took our furtive little pleasures like animals, be they rough sulphate swiftly sniffed, lager swigged hastily from the tin, or sex. Was it the speed or the breakneck tempo of our music which made punk sex so hasty, I wonder? When Johnny Rotten called sex 'sixty seconds of squelching sounds', he was unwittingly and amusingly pointing the dread finger of Bad in Bed at himself *and* his frantic *compadres*. They really didn't realise, bless them, that it didn't *have* to be that way.

The music papers had decided that there was this thing called the Big Five bands: the Sex Pistols, the Clash, the Damned, the Stranglers and the Jam. Actually, to anyone who *knew* – me and Tony, basically – there were of course only two groups who mattered, and they were the Clash and the Sex Pistols. Naturally, they hated each other; a lot like Oasis and Blur in the Nineties. And of course, while they were squabbling, another of the groups would pull themselves together, cut up on the inside and prove themselves to be more important than either of them – the Jam then (the Big Two never produced anything as brilliant as 'Eton Rifles'), Pulp now (ditto of 'Common People'). But that was in the future.

You had to choose, if you made it that far up the punk hierarchy (which was made actuality by where you sat on the stairs which led from the ground floor of the Roxy to the basement – no one lower than the Heartbreakers need apply. I usually sat on the seventh step, at the feet of Chrissie or Joe) whether you were with the Clash or the Sex Pistols. We were invariably with the Clash; all three of them had taken to Tony in a major way very early on, and whenever we were around they'd take it in turns to show their working-class solidarity with us by being vicious to Sebastian Conran. One night I walked up behind Joe without him knowing I was there and caught him holding forth to a gaggle of punk girl musicians: 'Don't knock 'er, right, because she's a good girl, Julie is . . . and nobody can make words dance like she can. Didn't you read 'er Silver Convention review?' The girl punks sneered jealously at me and I crept away, too stunned to speak. *I'm not worthy, Joe*!

Sometimes Tony and I would stay up all night with them in the studio, watching them through the glass door doing Capital Radio over and over again. I became so blasé about being there that often I would curl up on the leather couch and go to sleep with the sound of the young, raw, live Clash bouncing off the walls all around me; when I would wake up, Joe or Paul would have thoughtfully covered me with their leather jackets. Not Mick Jones, though; a true poseur, albeit a very sweet one, he always hung on to his, no matter how hot things got.

We had a good relationship with the Clash, an equal one more or less; this was envied by the other *NME* hacks, as it was definitely the exception which proved the rule. There used to be a lot of immature tittering – by middle-aged men who should have known better; 'middle-aged', where men are concerned, I'm afraid, means that they are equally distant from both the innocence of youth and the wisdom of age – about 'groupies' around the *NME* office. Nitpicker, delouse thyself, is all I can say to that. Because the *men* who work in the music business – be they hacks, DJs or record-label personnel – are groupies of the worst kind, in my experience. They don't even offer honest sex; they offer expense-account booze, or inferior drugs, to any zonked-out muso, however lowly, who will stop and share the moment with them. They don't expect the crooner in question to love them tomorrow, or even to recognize them; they are quite content to be used for a minute, so long as ONE OF THEIR FRIENDS sees them being so used. Forget groupies; these sycophants truly are the lowest of the low when it comes to the pop life.

But not all these men were promiscuous; sometimes it really was true love. Think, if you will, of Nick Kent; a serial rock monogamist if ever there was one. First it was Keith Richard, he of the precious vomit; then it was Johnny Thunders, who could oft be heard staggering around the Roxy claiming that Nick had given him 'a bad needle' – those boys must have had a sewing circle second to none, all the times this happened. But finally, Nick's flighty affections settled on Iggy Pop, whom he claimed to be 'like, blood-brothers' with from *way* back.

In the wake of English punk, after being called its godfather – grandfather, more like – more times than his record company could afford to ignore, Iggy was brought over to strut his tired old stuff one more time. Tony went off to interview him and bang, Iggy fell, like they all did. (All except *me*.) One day during his English tour when he had nothing to do, Iggy actually *called Tony at the office and asked if he could visit*! Tony, with magnificent ennui, said sure. And there he was; Mr Lock-Up-Your-Daughters meekly filling in a form at the security desk of IPC's King's Reach Tower in order to be given his visitor's pass.

Iggy stumbled nervously to the KinderBunker. He was a little fellow, I found, in all senses of the word. He looked like an utter American nerd; as he helpfully pointed out to Tony once, he resembled Alfred E. Neumann a bit. He squinted at me through thick glasses. 'Oh . . . hi.' He held out his hand.

'Tony's in the toilet.'

'Yeah . . . you must be Juuulie.' He said it in the long American way. Sounds even prettier that way, I find. Julie is a name only ever popular in France, Sweden and England; never in America. It's foreign to them, so they take great care with it. Pity old Iggy couldn't follow through on this (more dirt later), but anyway. 'Toneee's told me a *lot* about you.'

My heart sank. Bloody hell! It was true! He was A Man Obsessed. I just *knew* he'd told Iggy Bloody Pop that I was His Girl, like in a Bruce Bloody Springsteen song.

Cue Old Tone himself, walking in through the party-coloured plastic strips which did duty as the KinderBunker front door, self-consciously adjusting himself as he always did. He looked at me guiltily the moment he clocked Iggy and I *knew* that I was right.

'Angel,' he said shiftily. 'Iggy . . . Jimmy . . .'

'Hmm. Yes, we've met,' I said pointedly, turning my back and getting stuck into the important task of shuffling some blank type-writing paper. Behind me I heard Iggy snap to it.

'Hi, Toneee!'

'Iggy . . . Jimmy,' said Tony, still thinking about me. Because Tony was one of the few people Iggy had asked to call him by his real name, but because the idea of ***IGGY POP*** was so neon in Tony's mind (like all of us), Tony settled on both forms of address and so invariably sounded as though he was introducing the fellow to himself.

The awkward silence was broken by a truly awesome and awful sight: Nick Kent had heard the voice of his beloved, and now his face appeared over the top of one of the KinderBunker partitions. With his height, long, quivering neck, pop eyes and wildly batting eyelashes, he looked like a junkie giraffe on heat. 'Iggy!'

'Uh . . . hi . . . Dick . . .' Iggy responded lamely. Nick blinked rapidly, like a junkie giraffe gobsmacked, and then loped round into the KinderBunker itself to greet his blood-brother, who appeared to have forgotten his name, properly.

I turned round and smirked at Tony as Nick drooled over Iggy. He flashed a smile back and breathed again. I did adore him, I *did*; when he was content to be a mate, not *my* mate. We sniggered in unison as Nick attempted to renew old acquaintance with the Iggster, who had eyes only for the New Look: Tony.

The punchline to this joke comes in Manchester, where Iggy had had Tony (and me) taken and set up in some style. After the show, at the hotel where we were all staying, I met Iggy's bitchy American girlfriend, Esther.

'Jimmy . . . you know what guys are like,' she yowled, like Fran Drescher in *The Nanny*, only not beautiful or talented. 'He's on the road . . . he sees a pretty girl . . . *any* girl' – glaring – 'and he comes on. It's what guys do . . . y'know?'

Why was she telling me? I wondered. All was made clear later in Iggy's suite. The four of us sat talking on a *chaise longue*. Tony got up and went to the bathroom. Iggy, as natural as breathing, swung his tiny feet on to my lap, leaned forward and suggested in a whisper something that could have got us both jailed in the state of Georgia. Esther looked on, as Plus Ones tend to do, pride-free.

I was used to the English punk scene where, no matter how swift the sex, we were, above all, *mates*. Shock and horror both must have shown on my face, as they were quickly reflected on Iggy's when he realised he'd knocked on the wrong door. Right on time, enter Tony, who with one glance took in the situation, grabbed my hand and made our apologies. In his room he paced and ranted all night about my nobility, my inherent prole blood royal, my *honour*. I listened, enthralled; I felt just like a beautiful Mafia sister from Mario Puzo's *The Godfather*. Just after sunrise he attempted, once again, to get his leg over, and just like the noble, honourable Mafia princess of the blood royal he'd convinced me I was, I wasn't having any.

As I've said, I've never seen the pleasure in *chasing* someone – it's like, *they don't want you*! Excuse me, but how can that *ever* be sexy? – but boy, Tony was into it. And the way he did it, it *was* kind of wonderful. Unlike most men, Tony recognised no superior male other than his father; he bowed no knee, he doffed no cap. When he saw Iggy Pop make a slipshod, automatic pass at me, he saw red – and it gave birth to a miracle of comedy worthy of a wised-up Marx Brothers grand finale.

After this incident, just before his final foregone-conclusion capital city triumph at the Hammersmith Odeon, Iggy came around looking for drugs to speed him up. Straight-faced, Tony slipped him a handful of dramatic-looking capsules, half red and half hundreds and thousands.

'And . . . they'll do the trick, Toneee?'

'Surely, Jimmy . . .' Tony patted the little guy on the round, stunted shoulder and stared, steely, at me. 'They'll do the trick.'

Well: of course, they were laxatives. Iggy Pop, idol of Babylon, godfather of punk. Untouchable, had been reduced to using – frequently – a bucket in the wings of the mighty Hammersmith Odeon on his triumphant final date.

The Hammer of the Gods was up and running, and he knew no mercy. He didn't know the meaning of the word 'No', come to that, but what the hell. As that great showman, Mike Todd, wrote on the billboard advertising one of his earlier entertainments: IT MAY NOT BE SHAKESPEARE – BUT IT'S LAFFS.

Having seen off the Iggster, Tony was hardly going to see Mickey safely across the road, now was he? For the past few weeks leading up to my eighteenth birthday I had been ignoring El Tone's ever-lengthening shadow and posturing around London with my sentimental sadist for all to see. Tony tried to imply that all my punk confrères thought I was a right *slag* for taking up with an ancient hippie, but I laughed in his face; the punks, the important ones, adored Mickey because *he'd been there* in spades, annoyed the police and been busted from here to kingdom come, and been to jail for what he believed in (punks and hippies both were oddly non-specific on this one, especially to my highly political ears; you couldn't get a roach-clip between them on most matters *including*, as it shamefully turned out, *smoking dope*) and *you could hear him on a bloody MC5 record, couldn't you though but*!

These boys *idolised* the MC5. So once more, heh heh heh, seems *I'd picked the right flavour again, didn't it, El Tone*? He was a useless old drunk, sure, and didn't even *pretend* to be good in bed; next to him, though, men who were interested in being good in bed seemed rather frantic and undignified. It's a paradox, I've found, that being good at sex is actually not very sexy. It looks keen, and hearty, like being good at games. And invariably, with men who are almost *professionally* good at sex, you end up wanting your mother to write a note to get you off. Before *they* get you off, as it were.

Mickey's and my drunken experiments with flying in the face of Modern Nature came to a head one night a few days before my coming of age. El Tone was safely on 'the road' with Thin Lizzy or some such bunch of wild grandads who should have known better, but several days later when he returned to the Bunker my arms were still a living rhapsody in black and blue. Of *course* I was showing them off in a natty white cap-sleeved number; it was Indian summer and I was sweltering. (And seventeen, and silly, and a show-off, and *desperate* to be decadent.) Tone stood there, glowering, almost a year of lust and frust beamed at me like the light from an alien spaceship. Which he might as well have been, for all I understood him. Really, we'd only slept together the once – what exactly was his problem? Of course I knew; it was me. I was the problem and the solution both; when that happens, I guess they call it love.

'What's that?' He pointed rudely.

'What?' I looked around the Bunker perkily.

'That. On your arms.'

'Oh.' I stared at them. 'That.'

I looked him in the eye and then, perhaps foolishly, I laughed.

'Right!' Tone ripped into action, strode to his desk, picked up a twelve-inch blue vinyl record and thrust it towards my face. 'Read that!'

'Manufactured in . . .'

'Not that! *The title!*'

I peered. '"Prove It!"'

'Yes!' he yelled jubilantly. He then peeled off his wristwatch. 'Hold that!'

'Why?'

'Oh, for fuck's sake, Angel!' He was looking well hot and bothered. And he hardly *ever* swore in front of Angel (me). What in the name of Mike and for the sake of Pete was he about to do?

A scream and a crash from the hippie enclosure next door gave tongue to my childish fears and I ran in to see my beloved (Mickey) sprawled inelegantly on the floor, a bin on his Isro and blood on his mouth. Charlie was doing his best to hold a raging El Tone back and Jah Spence was making a real meal of this little crisis-slash-drama. At last! All his warnings about dem-fast-powders-gwan-make-you-slow had come to fruition! Ignore the fact that, for almost a solid year on speed we'd been brilliant and become famous, and in the same amount of time, smoking his interesting cigarettes, he'd continued to lose hair, cred and brain cells as though they were going out of fashion.

'She's not your girlfriend! *She's not your girlfriend*!' he kept jabbering at Tone, who didn't contradict him, merely looked mutinous and struggled to break free of Charlie's restraining arms, no doubt in order to inflict further GBH on my tousled sweetie.

I wondered if I should go to Mickey's aid. I wanted to, sort of, but there was a chance that this might inflame my protector even further. Anyway, he looked sort of stupid lying there with the bin on his head – it put me off a bit. And besides, I reasoned incredibly to myself, think of all the demos and stuff he was in in the Sixties! All the times he went down under the ruthless hooves of the mounted police, persecuting their very own people for having the guts to stand up to Uncle Sam's reign of Fascist terror in South-East Asia!

He's *used* to lying on the floor bleeding, I reasoned.

Charlie released Tone and he ran from the room, out of the office, slamming the door. All eyes fell on me, giving me what I believe is called an 'old-fashioned look' in triplicate. I sauntered as casually as I could past them and back into the KinderBunker, my one and only home. I sat on my desk, dangling my legs like an innocent ten-year-old, and I couldn't help but smirk. My dream had come true; I really and truly was, at the age of seventeen, a fully-fledged *femme fatale*.

So two weeks later, just after my eighteenth birthday, I was engaged to be married to one Tony Victor Parsons, pugilist of this parish, and less than a year after that I was living in a maisonette in Billericay, Essex. Yes, exactly – you tell me, guv!

I suppose what it *does* go to show is that you can take the girl out of the dead end, but you can't take the dead end out of the girl. My life as a bitch – free, amoral and incandescently happy – had lasted less than a year. And my life as a dog was about to resume in earnest.

CHAPTER ELEVEN

Housewife Superstar –
How to Stay Married for Exactly
as Long as You Want to

Love and marriage, went the song, go together like a horse and carriage. Well, I'm sorry, but in my experience that's not *quite* strictly true. It would be nearer *my* experience of the truth, actually, to say that love and marriage go together like angel cake and anthrax; that is, not at all. In fact, the only way I can see *any* resemblance to said mode of transport is (a) marriage is full of shit and (b) it's totally out-dated. *There's* your horse and carriage, if you like.

The first time I married for friendship; the second time I married for love. They both turned to ashes in my hands, crashing down in blood and sand. I remember once, very unhappy, burying my wedding ring on Brighton beach at four in the morning, because to wear it was no longer an honour but a sentence that soon must end or become the last chapter in my life. I went back to bed beside my husband at the Metropole Hotel and dreamed of a wedding-ring tree springing from the shingle and the rings turning into bullets on the branches. I woke up screaming.

And yes, I *know* what you're thinking, but *both* the characters I married went on to form perfectly unhappy relationships with other people with no help at all from *moi*. So it *wasn't* all my fault, thankyouverymuch!

When I say marriage, I suppose I mean domesticity; I'm sure that couples who have been shacked up together for a long while without benefit of a marriage licence feel just as often that one morning, ostensibly like any other, when they're taking out the garbage *they're taking out the remains of love in that black plastic bag, too*. I'm sure that long-term live-in lovers (live-in lover; surely an oxymoron), too, realise one day that they've got seven rooms to themselves in which they could easily have sex at any time of the day without being disturbed. And yet they have it less often in a week than they used to during a day – in the past, when they had *nowhere to go to have sex*. Seven rooms of gloom, just like the Four Tops said.

This is the great secret of modern love life, the great Fact of Life that no one tells you about at school, or at home, or behind the bike sheds; that IT WEARS OFF. This great lie that domestic sex lasts is responsible for more divorce, when it turns up unexpectedly, than any one other factor, I'm sure. Even snoring.

There is now, on the contrary, a massive brainwashing drive on the part of everyone from sex doctors to advertising agencies to deny this sad but obvious fact. The likes of Dr Ruth Westheimer pretend that you can 'keep sex alive in marriage'. Excuse me, but who wants to have sex with something that's been kept alive artificially? Have you seen *Frankenstein's Monster* recently? I love it how in Hollywood, whenever a couple are celebrated by the popular press for keeping their marriage 'hot' by sending each other dirty faxes or booking into a hotel without the kids, within six weeks *she's* been found with a sixteen-year-old boy extra and *he's* been found with a pot-bellied pig. This is Smug Fuck's Law. Don't be smug about fucking and how much your partner still loves it. Because it'll turn out that they've been faking it for the past three years, heh heh.

Then you see these car commercials where you've got these disgusting married couples smirking about the fact that they're having sex with each other. And this filth is being beamed straight into people's homes with no warning *at all* and kids are seeing it! And how do you think that makes kids feel, the idea that their parents are having sex? *Sick*, like it always does, like it's meant to.

Yet 'keeping your marriage hot' has become a modern

commandment – to the great detriment, it must be said, of marriage itself. *You* try keeping something hot for fifty years longer than it's meant to be hot – why, half an hour of keeping something hot will render most dinners dry, joyless and unappetizing. So it is with marriage and with sex in general: when it's hot it's hot, when it's not it's not and all the legwork, spadework, handwork and dickwork in the world won't bring the poor beast back to life and turn him into beauty. The beauty and the beast are both dead; that's why marriages fail.

I personally know of four happy marriages: those of Mr and Mrs T.W. Burchill of Bristol; Mr and Mrs V. Raven of Preston Park, East Sussex; my Auntie Dolly Brain and her ever-hunky husband Harold; and Annette and Colin Underwood of Brighton. That's it, then. For the rest – be they famous marriages which disintegrate over a thousand-day smorgasbord of recrimination in words and pictures, or simply a middle-aged couple glimpsed at a wedding, her smile frozen while he hisses in her ear 'Do you know what a very, very *stupid* woman you are?' – the great majority of marriages seem to me to be a vale of tears wrapped in a sea of loneliness. Fine for a day trip, but you wouldn't want to live there.

A marriage licence – as well as rendering sex effectively castrated from that moment on, for who wants to do something that you need a licence to do once you've got one? – is, as I have already said, equally a licence to kill. But even those good Englishmen whose homes are not their harems, dungeons and torture chambers, who do not rape their daughters, sodomize their sons and kill their wives for complaining about it, often take the licence then at *least* as a licence to ill.

It is the terrible eroding of courtesy in marriage that is the real killer; the creeping, sleeping sickness, the sleep of please and thank you and let *me* do that. I have known women married to men who were the very new model army of chivalry and courtesy in public – helping women with pushchairs on to buses and men with crutches across the road – who would then go home and abuse their wives, physically and/or verbally, for no reason other than that they were in a foul mood (probably exhausted from helping all those women on to buses and men across roads, come to think of it). Men routinely treat their wives in a manner that would have them locked away in jail or a mental ward if they tried it with a complete stranger. When men pick on complete strangers, we call them psychopaths and lock them away; when they pick on their wives and children, we call them 'domestics' and say they pose no risk to the public, but surely someone who can show cruelty to the people he is alleged to love above all others is *far* madder and more dangerous than someone who is nasty to a stranger, who is by definition someone they have no feelings for.

It is totally accepted by society, and even enshrined in supposed love songs, that 'you always hurt the one you love'. But why? – this is the logic of the lunatic asylum. Yet I know it to be true. I have known of a marriage in which the husband, a paragon of New-Man charm to the outside world, viciously beat up his wife for 'not being a good enough feminist'. And when it was over and he had to look at her black-and-blue face day in, day out, he reasoned this away by explaining that women 'are far stronger, and better, than men. We're weaker than you. So really, I didn't do such a bad thing.' I have known another marriage wherein the wife, suffering from amphetamine-induced psychosis, sobbed her little heart out for three solid days, day and night, curled in a cosy chair, clutching a child's stuffed toy – an orange knitted cat – for comfort. Her husband, similarly drugged and obsessed with the idea of being cool, did not ask her once what was the matter or offer one word of consolation. I am not necessarily saying that either of these marriages was mine. But I was there.

Bertolt Brecht, in a poem about Los Angeles, said that it did a unique thing: it doubled as both Heaven and Hell, Heaven for the rich and Hell for the poor. This is, in fact, an understatement; it is true of many great cities. It is also true of marriage, except that marriage is, on the whole, Heaven for men and Hell for women. Every survey ever done, no matter what its bias, invariably comes up with the same league table of physical and mental health. Married men first; single women second; married women third; single men last. If marriage had not existed, men would have had to invent it. *Which they did.*

To make women buy into this most unequal of opportunities, men had to fashion a tender trap. One element was the Big Frock, of course, and the champagne bash: The Most Beautiful Day Of A Woman's Life. As I've pointed out in the early ranting bit of this book (as opposed to the mid-section and conclusion ranting bits, *but no one forced you to read it, did they?*) it is one of the sickest jokes the patriarchal society has ever played, and continues to play, on women: to treat them like a princess for a day, before handing them a life sentence as a drudge – Cinderella in reverse, in fact, which is probably why this fairy-tale remains so achingly popular.

In the wedding of Lady Diana Spencer to Charles 'Scum' Windsor, this sick joke was taken to its logical, no-expenses-spared, no-holds-barred conclusion when a young woman raised on romantic fiction and unimpeachably, irreproachably in love offered up to her husband – in front of the whole wide world – not just her physical virginity but her true faith. And in front of the whole wide world, this man – a prince, a man wearing medals, the heir to the throne of our country and the next apparent head of our Church, God help us – stood there in the sight of the Lord and straight-faced made more of a fool of this young woman, this Diana Spencer, this precious pearl made girl, than any bully has ever made of any victim. We are used to seeing our beautiful icons – Marilyn Monroe, Martin Luther King, Lee Harvey Oswald – perish at the hands of Satan's slaves; in Diana – this Sloane alone, this Prisoner of Wales – the assassination was beamed live around the world. She was taken to Westminster Abbey in a glass coach and promised love. Next morning she awoke as the terrified, bewildered hostage of the strangest, cruellest, most dysfunctional dynasty since the Borgias.

Most marriages are not as blatantly deceitful and horrific as the one which was perpetrated by the House of Windsor upon the Lady Diana Spencer, but they are nearly all a gigantic con. And the lies men tell in order to ensure women's continuing collaboration with this risible state of affairs are cleverly and constantly changing. If men put as much effort into searching for a cure for cancer as they do into conning women into marriage, millions now living would never die.

In the old days, women married in order to live, because men lied to them about their inability to earn a living. Then they married because men lied to them that people would have no respect for them if they proved themselves unable to 'get' a man. But, as the amazing monstrosities endlessly waddling down the aisle bear witness, any woman can get a man. The real trick is TO GET AWAY.

These days it's more complicated. Men read depressing surveys which invariably conclude that the vast majority of women – even in France – would rather shop than shtup. And they know that women love to get a bargain and enjoy beating other women to a coveted item. Look at the queues for the Boxing Day sales! So this time around, the old lies about starving to death or dying of humiliation if you don't land a man have been cast aside and a new, more consumer-orientated approach tried: YOU'D BETTER GET A MAN QUICK – THEY'RE REALLY HARD TO GET.

Anyone who has been a teenage girl will know that the initial acquisition of a boyfriend has far more to do with the serious business of gaining the respect of other girls than with anything as banal as the vagaries of passion; heterosexuality is, in the first instance, little more than a fashion statement, as bisexuality will become later on. When a young girl gets herself a boyfriend, she is not so much obeying the call of the wild to fulfil her biological imperative as issuing a mating call to a girl gang of her choice: look what *I've* got, I'm *cool*, can I be with you? From the word go, from mother to peer group to best friend, men would be shocked and horrified if women were ever callous enough to reveal in full how peripheral men are to their lives. The rise of the single mother is merely the latest expression of this old, old instinct.

So consider what men now boast about as their ultimate Unique Selling Point. It used to be that we'd be ruined without them; physically, morally, spiritually. All of this hype has, at last, over a million years and through forces as diverse as feminism, Capitalism and aerobics, been blown away, leaving men with one reason why we want them: *There's not many of us left! We're rare, we are! Get one now, while stocks last!*

In pursuit of this most pathetic of reasons to exist, men have cooked up the usual ham-fisted cassoulet of lies about themselves and their importance, often with the help of stupid, masochistic and gullible women. The famous *Newsweek* headline about a single woman over the age of thirty-five having more chance of being assassinated than married was a plain and simple lie, cooked up by an idle sub one slow morning. It remains an issue of some shame to American journalism (a profession almost completely composed, by the way, of po-faced pedants, proof-readers and fact-checkers who tend very much to look down upon the cut-and-paste, slash-and-burn slapdash sauciness of the English press) that *Newsweek* had no problem with printing this headline – which to this very day is repeated as an actual fact by numerous journalists, ad-men and hackademics – whereas in an advertisement it would have been completely illegal.

There are, in fact, more than five per cent extra men of marriageable age in the USA, and only slightly fewer here. In London, there are apparently some 30,000 spare men between the ages of eighteen and forty-five whom no one wants to have sex with; on Friday nights you can find them in the Groucho Club. *Obviously* there's a whole bunch of spare men; the shops are full of wank magazines, the phone booth walls are crammed with names and telephone numbers of hookers and the Lonely Hearts columns speak of handsome, sensitive, multi-millionaires who are really good at cunnilingus, according to them. I have no idea where all these desperate women you're always reading about who would do anything for a boyfriend are but I personally don't know one woman under the age of sixty-five who can go down to the corner for a pint of semi-skimmed without coming back engaged. I *mean* it. Look at *me*! – I never wanted to get married. *It just happens*. Like getting overdrawn.

Then there are the rules. That book by those two American broads about how to get your man. Now I don't want to be a bitch and I don't want to diss a sister. But if I looked, dressed and sounded like the pair of screaming mimis who wrote that book – play dumb, don't speak, never argue and YOU WILL GET YOUR MAN! YES! HE MAY BE A SYPHILITIC WINO JUNKIE WITH SKID MARKS ON HIS TIE, BUT YOU WILL GET HIM – I, too, would be wondering why no man wanted to date me. It's very simple, girls. It doesn't need a book. It's called *charm*. Which, between you, me and the doorpost, American women don't have a whole way too much of. Please, ladies, have some of mine! Because my problem is I've got *way* too much. I'm a charm fountain, a charm mountain, a charm alarm. My brain is like a charm bracelet, only bigger and with more stuff hanging off it. For women like me, feminist *fatales*, as we reach the end of the century, the problem isn't getting your man. It's *escaping*. They're desperate, they are, those people with the extra leg. And they're coming after us *right now*. In the privacy of his own loony brain, every single man is a stalker.

It's a jungle out there, I tell you. And we're *still* the prey. I don't ever want to get divorced from my second husband. Because if I did, I'd marry the man I love. And then, after a period somewhere between five and ten years, I'd get bored with him. And he wouldn't get bored with me, because they don't, and I'd go ahead and cause 57 varieties of heartbreak. And I don't want to do that again.

So at last I have it: the whole point of modern marriage and its sole recommendation. If you're married to someone you've stopped loving you leave them, but you stay married to them. Because then, and only then, do you not get married to the person you love. And the person you will then grow to loathe. Because love, as I've said, *is* a lemming.

As the rules say, if you can be bothered to break sweat you can make any man fall in love with you, and marry you, too. The question is, then: why bother? For the 'Wedding March' is also the 'Dead March from Saul', only not as gorgeous and scary. Though in a way, scarier. Because it signals the willingness of two people voluntarily to murder their love. Well, *I've* got a rule, too. And mine is: Just say no. NO, NO, NO!

CHAPTER TWELVE

Ambition, Thatcher's Children and Me – The Eighties from the Inside

I'll tell you two good things about being in a lousy, used-up marriage, though: you get, finally, to take your make-up off every night and slather your face with a nice gooey night nourisher which for once isn't sperm. And you get a heck of a lot of work done. During my first marriage, of five years' duration, I produced four books; during my second marriage, of eleven years' duration, three. As you may be able to deduce from this, the sex was a lot better in the second marriage.

Workaholism? Hey, don't send *us* no doctor! Show me a workaholic and I'll show you someone who's keeping her nose to the grindstone and her shoulder to the wheel in order to avoid putting her mouth to the genitalia. Working late is the ultimate Get Off Sex Free card.

It's a fact that the Protestant work ethic got invented because Martin Luther couldn't stand doing it to Mrs Luther any more. And look at who's embraced it! The Swedes and the Italians, probably the most beautiful races on earth, don't work a minute longer than they have to, so they can have all that extra time off for fucking each other. The Japanese, probably the ugliest, work the hardest so they don't have to. And I bet you that at least nine out of ten so-called 'workaholics' are married. Like I was.

*

You might or might not have noticed that I've got a bit of a thing about sex. So much of a bit of a thing, in fact, that I've never been able to do it the way other people do. It's not that I can't master any of the positions or anything; rather, it's my sexual speeds that seem to differ.

I've got two sex speeds: Mad For It and Why Bother? Whereas most people are apparently striving for and happy with the national average of 2.5 times a week (and that's higher than in other countries!) I can only do it three times a day or not at all. I can recall several points in my life when I have gone into what can only be called sexual hibernation, like a tortoise.

When I first saw that 2.5 statistic I thought it must be a misprint for 25. When I realised it wasn't, I felt extremely dismayed. There is something about the idea of having sex 2.5 or even three times a week which makes me want to scream violently, run down the street tearing my clothing and hack out my primary and secondary sex organs. It's just so *blahhhhh*. When you want someone, you want them all the time; when you don't want them, *you don't want them*. So why bother? Show me someone who's having it 2.5 times a week and I'll show you a person who's keeping the peace with a long-term, burned-out partner by offering a piece every few days. It's just horribly sad. No wonder people get post-coital triste if that's the way they carry on.

What's the best definition of a liar? Someone who says they still REALLY REALLY love sex with the same person after doing it regularly with them for more than four and a half years.

As popular songs tend to show, we desperately want to believe that love lasts longer than a bad verruca. I'm not so sure, myself; I feel it far more likely that a song from the perspective of, say, 'Hello, I Love You' is far more likely to be honest than a song which claims 'I Love You As I Loved You When You Were Sweet Sixteen'. Unless, of course, he wrote the song the night of her seventeenth birthday.

During my three years at the *NME*, I was flash, amateurish, out of my box on sulphate, unable to hold the most basic conversation with record company personnel – in fact, I could barely function as a grown-up. But I also brought a degree of innocence and integrity to the paper that was unheard of; I wasn't interested in ligs, or freebies, or expenses, or all those other things that ruin writers. The *NME* reached new heights of both sales and credibility, and quite naturally one's own fame grew. European camera crews would frequently follow one up to the office, where they would hang around waving their booms in people's faces and generally getting in the way. One's colleagues were not amused. But the jealous jibes of the geek chorus were not my main preoccupation. A birthday was looming – the Big One.

Twenty.

It's very nice being a cult figure when you're young – there was a badge made of me in the Temporary Heroes series, which says it all – but once you hit twenty, it pales; being a cult figure, compared to mainstream fame, is like being asked to someone's house for cocktails when you know all the other guests are staying for dinner.

I had three good years at the *NME*, but by 1979 pop was lying fallow and through its teeth again. All around me men of thirty were still looking for The Word in a spinning plastic platter. 'Is there life after *NME*?' they'd ask after they had one too many lemonade shandies, before doddering off to addle their brains even further with help from the demon weed. A few inhalations later and if it was your lucky day you'd be treated to a maudlin roll-call of selected lost souls who'd taken that long walk out into the real world and never returned through the IPC portals: OD, nervous breakdown, mental shakedown, collared by God Squad (Eastern bald branches rule), house-painting, *working for a record company*! (Weren't we *all*, I'd sometimes mutter cynically.) So they stayed at the *NME*; it was their Shangri-La, with drugs on, and they seemed to believe that within its walls they would stay forever young.

For myself, crumbling to dust was a chance I had to take; you can sink or swim in the mainstream, but all you'll ever do in the margins is tread water. I could see no point in preaching to the converted for the rest of my unnatural life. And so at twenty I was working for *The Face*, at twenty-three for the *Sunday Times* and at twenty-six for the *Mail on Sunday*.

In those days, writers from the pop papers didn't write for the proper papers, mainly because no one ever asked them to. And in the Eighties I was criticized a great deal by my erstwhile colleagues for 'selling out', a charge I found ironic on two counts. One, that the *NME* was owned by Reed International, which had considerable holdings in apartheid-ruled South Africa, and two, that the very people most enthusiastic and energetic about levelling this accusation at me have since then been breaking all known rim-job records trying to get into Fascist, racist, imperialist Fleet-Street-as-was. They must be pushing fifty now, and most of them are *still* not trusted to write about anything but pop; Neil Spencer, hysterically, is the proud author of a weekly horoscope column. No wonder they hate me.

That same resentment which routed me from my West Country home – that I was *too clever by half* – I finally found in London, too, among people who should have known better. I was a Thatcherite Bitch, I began to hear half-way up the Eighties, which is middle-class no-mark for a working-class girl who just so happened to have the guts to make it. I'm very much afraid that white middle-class no-marks like their proles and their women the way they like their blacks: down and out of their element and in need of Massah's help, confirming all their worst fears about the big, bad market-place. Well, they can take their frigging First Aid boxes and minister to some other bitter-sweet young thing from the wrong side of the tracks because I refuse to lose. I will not be anyone's hard-luck story. Coming from where I did, the most rebellious thing I could have done was to make it big. And I did.

When in doubt, pout; that had always been my philosophy. But I was having difficulty keeping a stiff upper lip as I sat across from my agent at lunch in the Groucho Club that spring afternoon in 1988.

The menu? Me, me and me, followed by small, mint-crisp morsels of *moi* with the coffee. My career was at a crossroads, my rent was in the red and my status was at a standstill, stuck at two million readers per week. So I said, as I toyed with my *nouvelle cuisine* portion of unwaged minority person: 'Anthony, what should I do next?'

'Well, Julie – have you ever thought of writing fiction?'

'You mean a *novel*?' Novel; that's the word we hacks revere above all others, like Italians do 'mother'. Hey – I've fucked ya novel! That's the worst thing you can say to a hack.

I visualise something precious, something perfectly bound in purple . . . and what's it about? It's about . . . ninety pages should do the trick, I reckon. Nice big type and plush paper – dead thick. Lush.

'Well, why not? I was speaking to the head of fiction at Pan the other week and *she* said—'

'Pan? But they're . . . You mean . . .'

'A blockbuster! Yes! Why not?'

'Why *not*? Why, you miserable little bloodsucker – I've never been so insulted in my *life*!' Heads turn. 'How much?' I hiss furtively.

'Thanks. The lady will have my head on a platter, and some Beaume de Venise to wash it down with,' my agent is telling the waitress as he hands back the dessert menu. He turns back to me and smiles like Judas selling someone a second-hand car. 'A six-figure advance, easily. And that's just in England. Just in hard-back.'

'I've never been so insulted in my life,' I repeat thoughtfully. But I have, actually. My last three books have been what is known in mixed company as 'cult successes'. Which means flops. Which is an insult, three times over.

'Well, think about it!' my agent calls as I exit from the down-stairs brasserie at a canter. I do. By the time I get home I've got a plot, a heroine and a first paragraph. Take *that* to the bank!

And so I came to write a blockbuster novel, though at 300 pages it was something of a bulimic blockbuster. Never mind; the meat of the matter was all there – shopping, fucking and bitching *bons mots*; it was only the reams of meticulously researched details about life on a Malayan rubber plantation at the turn of the century (the sort of thing other, older, rather self-loathing blockbuster writers insist on putting in to prove they're 'real' story-tellers) that I left out.

I always loved blockbusters when I was growing up, ever since I read *Valley Of the Dolls* at twelve (same year as I read *Lolita*) and thought, *Yesss, that's* the life! (I suppose I saw it as a sort of how-to self-help manual, which apparently it isn't.) Just after *Ambition* came out, *everyone* said they'd always loved blockbusters, the way they all claimed that they'd seen Va Pistols at the Screen on the Green in 1977. And as we all know, if everyone who claims they'd been there really *had* been there, the Screen would have had to have been the size of Shea Stadium. But I have proof of my devotion: the first great blockbuster essay, published in the *NME* in – wait for it – 1979. First on the (writer's) block again, boyzzz.

'Too much sex, not enough pages,' said one American publisher; 'I wouldn't let my *secretary* read this, let alone my mother,' said another; 'I felt the table move,' said my paperback publisher after finishing the manuscript. It was the prospect of writing sex scenes that terrified me, I must say; greater men than I have fallen at this fence and limped away from Bonker's Brook looking like right prannets.

But I was pleased with the sex in *Ambition* and, after a brief – and, I believe, becoming – period of bashfulness actually put in *too much*. When W. H. Smith were given the manuscript to approve, they actually requested three cuts before they would stock it. These were (a) watersports ('But they're in *love!*' I protested to my editor. 'That makes it *worse*,' she scolded), (b) a girl having two men at once (sheer sexism; blockbusters are peppered with two men having two girls at once – which is, when you think about it, a much less *practical* arrangement) and (c) anal sex between girls (this is the one that invariably makes people say, 'But how?' *Suckers!*) I made the cuts, because I believe in censorship just for the hell of it – true art will always find a way; no one swore in *White Heat* or *Little Caesar*, but they were better gangster films than *Goodfellas* – but I still feel that double standards were applied here,

just because I was so darn young and cool and obviously not
'respectable'. I mean, those things are kinkier than getting stuffed
with a *goldfish?* Not in my house, they're not.

It's hard to credit that, in the Nineties, people actually craved and
celebrated an Eighties revival; several, actually. Because no decade
in the post-war world has had such a bad press from both high-
brows and hip. At least the 'conformist' Fifties had Frankie Sin
and the dry Martini, the 'messy' Sixties had the mini and the
Mods, and the 'apocalyptic' Seventies had Biba lipstick and the
sound of Philadelphia.

But the Eighties were lost on us, buried beneath the clichés of
carping hacks and the duck-billed platitudes of playwrights pissed
off with the fact that squatting in the mud at 'festivals' went out of
style. Its salient images all speak with Biblical portent of moral
decline and the worship of Mammon and mammaries; Samantha
Fox on the floor of the Big-Bang-Day Stock Exchange would have
been the perfect Eighties photo opportunity. Greedy City boys,
selfish Yuppies, smug Sloanes, post-modern towers of Babylon
and inhuman 'isms' by the score: worra life, eh?

I walked with another Eighties, however; a kid with one eye on
the mirror and the other on the main chance. Status-conscious, yes
– but bad, uncaring, greedy? Nah – neither a saint nor a sinner, just
someone tired of being on the right-on, street-cred ropes with her
nose pressed up against Langan's window-pane, graced with a bit
of talent and a lot of front and a desire to move on up.

What made the Eighties culturally unique was that for the first
time the dichotomy and division between Hip (marginal; in the
know and in the red) and Cube (mainstream; on the make and in
the money) finally ended with the two sides falling into each
other's armistice. Hip wanted the cash and career that only the
Cube could provide; Cube wanted the kudos in return. And anyway, this opposition had always been more of a theological neces-
sity than a reality; there were always those at the sharp end of Hip
who knew that if they didn't move into the mainstream PDQ it
would be fifty years of hard labour treading water at the *NME* or

ZTT. The Eighties simply stopped speaking with forked tongues – and got the knives out.

Things Which Seemed Like a Good Idea at the Time but I've Gone off Now
- My husbands
- Red China
- Feather cuts
- Writing on your arm in biro
- Cunnilingus
- The Latin Hustle
- Talking in a baby voice during sex
- Stealing
- Saying 'Absolutely'
- 'Always and for ever'
- Foreign objects
- Subsidising small magazines
- Sex in your swimming pool in broad daylight while overlooked on three sides by neighbours who are at home during the day
- Making promises you can't keep
- Keeping promises
- Faking orgasms
- Mrs Thatcher
- The Millennium
- Borrowing medication
- Having sex three hours after an abortion
- Jimmy The Hoover
- Putting all your eggs in one basket
- Opening that can of worms
- Kicking over the traces
- Bending over backwards
- Going the whole hog
- One for the road
- All you can eat
- Whippings
- Ponces

- Footless tights
- Being a 'sexy bitch'
- Class reunions
- Class envy
- Club class
- Club sandwiches so big they have to be held together with a stick
- Visible lovebites at the age of thirty-seven
- A frank and free exchange of views within a healthy marriage
- Spending £569 on a Dolce Gabbana rucksack and it's too young for you by a long chalk and you have to give it to Charlotte R.

I suppose I should mention money here. As I write, I'm overdrawn at the bank. I won't say how much, but if you saw it written down, you'd think it was a sex chatline number. Yet *Ambition* sold more than a million copies and just two years ago I was earning £130,000 a year at the *Sunday Express. You* go figure, guv. I suppose the problem is that when you come from No Money, no money is what you end up with. Look at Pools winners, like Viv Nicholson. *That's* the way I've lived my life. When you come from No Money, all money seems like Monopoly money and you don't take proper care of it. You lose it down the back of the sofa. You buy presents for people without bothering to look at the price. You get married. Before you know it, it's all gone.

You wouldn't *believe* some of the hopeless, useless, excuseless causes and characters I've squandered my money on. Someone should have stopped me and had me committed until I calmed down a bit. To beggars in the street alone I must have given away thousands of pounds in the space of twelve years. If any of them are reading this, incidentally, and remember me thrusting a fifty-pound note at them one dark night in Soho or Brighton between the years of 1984 and 1996 – I was the tall, dark, handsome piece of work with the bright eyes and the fan club – could they please send it back if they've still got it? Cheers!

Really, what was I *playing* at? The beggars are the very least of it. At least, being poor, you could say they deserved it. What I can't explain is the way I lavished my hard-earned cash on the undeserving bourgeoisie. Boys with titles, men with trust funds – and the funny thing was, I wasn't even trying to buy their attention, *that* old chestnut. I already had their blind devotion long before I started picking up the tab. Perhaps I was trying to buy their silence; to buy time. Whatever I was buying, I was paying well over the odds for it. Maybe, in some demented way, I had picked up from my dad the idea that having money was basically a dirty business and not *really* worthy of the proletariat blood royal. Whatever, I have always treated lucre as though it truly were filthy and might well leave a permanent whiff of ordure on my silky hands. 'Ugh – money, lots of it? Here – catch – *you* have it!' Truly, I divested myself of my money with all the single-minded glee of an obsessive-compulsive playing Pass the Parcel.

I was twenty-four in the summer of 1984, back in London after being married alive for half a decade in one of the many armpits of Essex; as armpits go, Essex is a veritable octopus. A far cry from the run-down, depressed, post-punk place I'd left, London was everything a great city should be: short-tempered, nasty and British. With *careers* again, careers starting to loom over the changing skyline like King Kong ravishing Manhattan.

Medialand and West Wonderland were being written up in the glossies and the Sunday supps, and both frothy fiefdoms revolved around the Groucho Club, which had just opened. Every night, a man would walk through the bar and into the dining-room, and the whole club would be hushed mid-bustle as a hundred eyes followed his progress. Then, as he vanished, a rippling whisper would sashay through the spritzers: '*That's the man who finished something!*'

In those years plans, projects, CVs and calling cards filled the Soho sky like tickertape greeting Charles Lindbergh. London had more egomaniacs, monomaniacs, nymphomaniacs, dipsomaniacs, dreamers and deranged than any city in the world, including New York. But what made it different, and special, and even lovable, was that most of the people playing the game were only half serious. The whole hustle was played out with a theatrical and self-conscious obsessiveness that verged on parody; we were playing Manhattan in the Fifties, with much talk of Losers, being Finished in this Town, being Wiped off the Board, and A Party and Mr Nobody with a One-Way Ticket to Nowheresville. Some people, of course, could not differentiate parody from viciousness; I'll never forget, in 1984, Toby Young introducing myself (a recent acquaintance) to a posse of Bright Young Oxford Things: 'This is Julie Burchill. She's the cleverest girl in London,' only to follow this by gesturing at my friend with the words: 'This is X. He's a loser.'

Happy days, then. We had all read *What Makes Sammy Run?* (Toby Young in fact lent it to an eighteen-year-old friend of his who handed it back a week later and said with a straight face that it was the best self-help–help-yourself manual he'd ever read) and we had all seen *Sweet Smell Of Success* so many times we were muttering 'Light me, Sidney!' in our sleep. But more than anything, we were McLaren's Children. We had all been dreaming teens when Malcolm's finest moment (*only* moment) was going through its paces and jumping through its hoops on prime-time slo-mo. This, much more than being Thatcher's Children – though they turned out to be very close indeed – would dog the rest of our lives. It could be summed up as a life-style and attitude which acknowledged that it had lost everything (the class struggle, real politics) that mattered but instead of weeping turned this into a cause for vicious celebration and an excuse for chasing material things with which to soothe our smarting, thwarted Spartan souls. Paul Smith, Katharine Hamnett, Rifat Ozbek; they all made variations on the same garment, which was a very expensive handkerchief with which to dry our eyes, put a shine on our shoes and go back to the Style Wars refreshed. There's a word that comes to mind, what is it? . . . ah, PATHETIC.

Ever since the mid-Eighties, desperate hippies with haircuts have tried to rewrite and reclaim punk as the last gasp of right-on rebellion. But it wasn't. It *was* rebellious – but only in the way that Mrs Thatcher was. Punk was about a break with consensus. And we media brats, like our susser soulmates who would come up a few years later in the City – the Big Bang boys, which in itself sounded like a Malcolm McLaren concept group, a lovely little earner on paper like Bow Wow Wow and She Sherriff, but positively *limping* when it was finally called upon to drag itself up to the microphone – were McLaren's *and* Thatcher's children. As the action moved from Roxyland to West Wonderland to EC Moneyland, we were still non-U upstarts with names like Steve and Paul and Julie and Debbie. And what we all shared was Attitude: short-haired, hyper-impatient, get-filthy-rich-quick, liberal-baiting and hippie-hating. This is what McLaren bequeathed to the world and it was enough. Forgive him his projects, for he knows not what he does, and creativity has become little more than a nervous tic for him. But he *was* our wet nurse and liquid gold ran from his scrawny breasts, and for this he deserves the respect you would give a mother. For in the Eighties, we were all McLaren's Children.

Those years were so important because they marked the last time that Hip was truly at home in the modern world. They rushed in where trad-Left and highbrow feared to tread – be bold, be bold, but not *too* bold! – celebrating the ephemeral, the possibilities and products of the new industries, the importance of style and taste, and the new freedoms offered by cultural confusion.

We were in freefall, no doubt about it. And a few truly modern souls, such as myself, revelled in the chance to live life at this most gorgeously chaotic of new frontiers, where nothing and no one seemed certain of anything any more, except that all money was Monopoly money now and that if you drank *only* vintage champagne you didn't get hang-overs. Oh, and that God was dead and Communism was over. (With the benefit of hindsight, I'd like to point out that only the second of these modern wisdoms has any truth to it whatsoever.)

But this attitude took a strong stomach and a stiff upper lip, and for the most part what passed for a modern hipster – mostly white and male – couldn't take it, fake it or really make it. There was a gradual realization that cultural freefall would have losers as well as winners; and, for the first time, and for a change, the losers looked highly likely to be white and male.

Well, we can't have that, now can we, John? It was amusing to watch how, suddenly, hipsters and right-ons alike became such fussy eaters, socially speaking, damn nigh leaving everything that came about after 1945 on the side of their plates for Mr Manners. Did we say we wanted freedom, mobility and change? – sorry, could we have continuity, community and conservation instead, please? Ta.

Whether it was that arch-snob John Mortimer, drivelling on about the glory days of the old-guard Macmillan government and their alleged *noblesse oblige*, or Baroness Warnock being made 'physically sick' by a television documentary which showed Mrs Thatcher buying off the peg at M&S, or the *Arena* Jocko Homo boys whingeing on in perfect parodies of A. N. Wilson (who had just announced his intention to vote Labour for a more stable, less changeable society), Whyohwhynia about the 'orrendous break-up of community and all these Yuppies being ALLOWED to buy PROPERTIES in CITIES (an AMAZING liberty, no? – especially when the self-same hacks were sitting on nice little earners in Hampstead (Jah Spence) and Highbury (El Tone); what in the world makes it sound for journalists from outside London, like these two, to come in and buy properties from indigenous Londoners, but not for bankers? Answers on a pinhead, please!), what it added up to was a bad case of the revisionisms and a new world view which owed a lot more to Prince Charles – let's keep things as they are and admit that those Moslem chappies talk *a good deal of sense* about women – than to Prince Nelson – let's tear the roof off the sucker and see what comes down, what sparkling splintery shards the human spirit will shine into.

Handy Pre-Millennial Household Tips: Feng Shui
The idiocy of the Nineties is best summed up by the fact that while people no longer appear to believe in something as logical and sensible as the Marxist analysis of our system and its suggestions for improving matters for the greatest number of people, they do on the other hand believe that moving the furniture around can change the course their lives will take. To me, there is

only one point in moving furniture around and that is to procure a spontaneous abortion. And I really do think that if you subscribe to the theory and practice of Feng Shui, you should have your vote kindly but firmly removed from you. Because if you believe that where you put a household plant can seriously change your life, for good or ill, then you have a lower IQ than said houseplant. And it should probably be telling *you* where to go. However, I fully realise that there may well be imbeciles, lunatics and morons reading this book, and for them I have included the following Feng Shui tips:

- Rarely, if ever, pour sump oil on the floor in the hallway just inside the front door. Callers may fall and injure themselves and slap a dirty great lawsuit on you and take all your money which will lead to your quality of life suffering profoundly.
- Try to refrain from hanging weights over the bed. They may well fall and bash your brains in and make you an imbecile, and you'll have to give up your day job and devote yourself to the ancient Chinese art of Feng Shui full time because you will be fit for nothing else.
- Do not paper your walls with banknotes. Casual callers may see them and inform criminals of their whereabouts.
- Never sexually mount a cactus. They are spiky as all-get-out.

Two maps of the modern world: for those at home in it, the map says *you are here* and that's all we need. For the frightened the map says, in the medieval manner, *here be dragonnes*. But how you gonna keep 'em down on the farm – sorry, 'rural community' – now that they've seen the Café de Paris?

From the great liners to the great bylines, the cry comes down this incredible, inedible century as we stare at the sun rising behind the Millennium Wheel of Fortune – *all aboard that's coming aboard*! Are *you* on for a one-way trip to the New World? No, things will *never* be certain again – no matter how much football you watch, or how many Richard Ford novels you read, or Thai bar girls you pay. You will never really know again, Little Man,

Little White Western Media Man, will you? You will never really *know*.

We are in a freefall now, for sure – and about time too, for it is the natural state of Capitalism. As a Communist, of course, I don't care for it or approve of it – but you can't have Capitalism with a safety net. *This is what it looks like. Suits you, Sir!*

The escape from community and continuity and Conservatism, the whole Holy Grail that the *Zeitgeist* of the Twentieth-Century Express sought as it screamed like a bolshy banshee from station to station, is here at last. Which is not to say that things are perfect – but to recognise the value of social and cultural changes that have and will continue to open up, evolve and flourish whatever the complexion of government. In England, in 1996, there was a common-or-garden case of obstruction brought to court when a young clubber, A, was accused by a young policeman, B, of obstructing his police car by insisting on leaving his own car door open while A ate a hamburger, which his friends – his girlfriend, her best friend and the best friend's boyfriend – objected to the smell of in their delicate post-rave state. The judge found against the policeman, and he and his clubbing contemporary left court to be comforted/celebrated by their own highly partisan supporters. What makes the case so poignant and so modern is that both policeman and clubber were black, and their witnesses on either side white. *That's* a beautiful face of the modern world, if you like; not a happy-clappy rainbow coalition, but a genuinely colour-blind, business-as-usual strop. People *choosing* their side – not being condemned by birth in it. We can all be cuckoos now. We don't *have* to go home, unless we want to.

Don't try to fight it, because you'll be the loser. People have dreamed and died and worked their minds to distraction to make us this lonely, this free, and the least we owe them is enjoyment. Because in order to change the modern world you must first learn to love it.

CHAPTER THIRTEEN

Escape from the Groucho Club – Brighton Rock and the Bristol Sound

'One bright night, gonna fly right out my window / Gonna fly so high in the night sky / That the people below won't see me go' – 'A Famous Myth' by J. M. Comanor.

Well, that's my story and I suppose that I can take it to the bank or tell it to the judge, depending on how you see stuff.

When I started this book, like everyone over the age of eighteen months I definitely had a few scores to settle. But flicking through my gorgeous volume I see that I've tried to shield whomever I could in any way I could from facing the public ridicule and contempt that would inevitably greet the full documentation of their callousness and stupidity; for any nasty thing I've said here, there's things a hundredfold more nasty just sitting out this dance in my Book Of Evil Thoughts, believe me! I don't know why I didn't put them in. I suppose it's because I feel sort of sorry for everyone who's ever been involved with me, no matter how fleeting the engagement. (Having said that, if they *should* be unpleasant from this moment on, I feel it only fair to inform them that my Book Of Evil Thoughts never sleeps. Only power-naps.)

Lots of people will think I'm a real bitch because I wrote this book; a real bitch, that is, because I barely mentioned them, nor even thought about them when I pondered over my life. They were waiting for some big denouement that they could at least sulk and simmer over, and at best sue against. But I just *can't*, I'm sorry, because you never meant that much to me, whoever you are. In our changing world, lots of people make their friends their family. But I've never wanted or needed to. I've got my parents and my sons, my boy and my Charlotte, and that's all I'll ever, ever need. It's an only-child thing. It's a sociopath thing. Whatever, suckers, *I'm* happy and *you're* not.

You know with those Nineties, and why I had to go, just like pop stars at the height of their powers just push off and everyone thinks they're mad? It's that you suddenly see yourself clearly and you hate it. And if you hung around, you know you'd become a really vile old sham, a shameless ham, like all the other scene-masters who've held the beat too long and bent it out of its original slinky, sinuous shape into something lumpen and clumping.

I still maintain that my reign as Queen of the Groucho Club was a glorious thing to live through – especially if you were me, the people I was tipping or the people who were poncing off me. YES, YOU! *Well* may you hang your head in shame! Oh – you weren't; you were looking for coke crumbs. Well, they're long since dried up, I think you'll find.

One thousand and one nights of fun under the boho Soho skies – a veritable smorgasbord, yes, of lines, women and shlong. But I'll tell you what went wrong with that life in the end, the West Wonderland media meteors life. Like I said, people held things a beat too long – like five years. And so people were still doing Eighties things, but with a Nineties, amockalyptic, puritanical attitude; that *was* wrong and, like, the decline of the Roman Empire, but hell, we'll do it anyway! Men go in particularly for this gutless, joyless approach to having a laugh, I often find; I can't recall the number of boys who've stayed up taking hundreds of pounds' worth of coke all night in my Bloomsbury rooms, only to collapse in a pool of tears as the sun comes up, and to curse the modern world and all that's in it. Talk about a waste of decent drugs! When I used to witness this, I felt real, righteous anger – like a mother who spends a fortune on fancy food for her brood, only to see them mess it about, build castles out of it and end up throwing it at each other.

People could have used those drugs to good ends! There's people *starving* for drugs all over the world! That a bunch of self-loathing middle-class mummy's boys had used up perfectly good drugs only to fuel their maudlin wallowing in their own mental effluent really got up my snout. For some reason girls don't tend to get self-loathing on drugs, probably because they're not as loathsome as boys. But they do usually want to plait your hair some time before sunrise, which is a bit of a pip.

You know what I was? I was like one of those brilliant-coloured pilot fish, surrounded by a host of insignificant parasites; dead-beat men, crap collagists and magazines which quickly turned form *magnifique* to *merde* when it emerged that the hands allegedly guiding them were more interested in masturbation than steering a true course. I suppose you know I'm talking about Toby Young here. Well I am, but only because he's symptomatic of that whole group of promising Eighties boys who just *didn't bother* to put in the required amount of effort it takes to produce a book, a script, a love that lasts.

When I met Toby in 1984 he was nineteen; blond, brilliant and far and away the cleverest, funniest boy I'd ever known. We became spiritual twins, closer than lovers. But people always warned me against him. 'Why are you dragging *that* around with you?' Robert Elms demanded at a *Face* party that year. Three years later in Marks & Spencer (Islington), his own mother told me he was evil and that I shouldn't waste my time on him. Ungrateful fool that I was, I furiously barged into her trolley with mine and waltzed off. I should have listened to her. I would have saved a lot of money.

When we fell out in 1995, he was bald, bilious and paying for sex. *And admitting to it*! He pretended he wasn't ashamed of himself, but I knew better. His father, Michael Young, wrote the 1945 Labour manifesto and created the Open University; his son paid for sex – that said it all, really. Talk about the Descent of Man! And of course, the punishment that Toby will take to the grave is not my rejection of him for a *girl*, but the fact that his mother and father must have been so dreadfully, grievously disappointed in their only son. Hi, Tobes!

In Toby I saw the first birth squeals of what was to become the Lad Culture, and because of Toby I can see that the whole *Loaded* thing is based on self-loathing. I mean, *I know* those boys; I've made toast for them at four in the morning after a heavy night of ping-pong and coke, and I've had to ask James Brown to leave my flat when he *just wouldn't stop* asking a black friend of mine where he 'came from'.

And as I've said, such men have reasons enough to loathe themselves. Take the Lad obsession with sport. It is, interestingly, a fact that many women will confirm that men who are over-interested in sport – boxing and football especially – are crap at sex; in Italy, of all places with *no* reason to lie about such a sacred subject, doctors have proved that playing the beautiful game too much makes the ugliest part of a man's agenda shrink quite dramatically. This may be cause, effect or your good old chicken-and-egg situation – I do not know, as I do not know so many things.

But, this being a free(ish) society, Jocko Homos *know* that the women they sleep with have probably been on the receiving end of some other rod – some of them belonging to men who knew how to use them too. In London in the early Nineties, at the height of the New Laddism and football craziness both, it was well known among the narrow-hipped broads on the London media scene that the only man at the Groucho Club worth getting horizontal with was a young critic called Tom Shone. You just *knew* that Tom was brilliant in bed because the minute the talk turned – as it invariably did – to matters sportif, Tom would yawn, down his vodkatini in one and say loudly 'God! I *hate* sport! Especially *football*! Why would *anyone bother* once they'd left school?' And all the girls would turn into steaming vats of oestrogen and draw straws in the Ladies' Powder Room about who was going to go home with him that night. (Tom Shone, in the first flush of extreme youth, was my prettiest boy protégé ever: a drinking, thinking man's Daniel Day-Lewis. He used to keep bringing his girlfriends round to my flat for inspection, and invariably I'd make a big fuss of them so that he'd get jealous and go off them. At one point he kept bringing back girls called Helen and I said a really bitchy, clever thing to my teenage *compadre* Emma Forrest about them: 'Always a Helen, never a Helena.')

And if you're a Jocko Homo, and you *know* you're a damp squib in the sack, you can't stand the thought that a woman prefers someone else sexually to you; it makes you see red. So when O. J. Simpson, Michael Tyson or Paul Gascoigne kills, rapes or slaps a woman who has rejected them, they do it for their fans as well – as surely as they land that punch or score that goal. Sport has become a continuation of the sex war for men who are not man enough to see a woman stand on her feet without feeling a burning desire to knock her on to her knees; all the better to make her unable to realize how short they are. And such sportsmen are sad but suitable icons for what I must conclude is an actual Lost Generation of men; a generation who have refused to learn the best things either their fathers or feminism could have taught them. And as we thirtysomething, glittering bitches, your lapdogs no longer, flounce off with our girlfriends, our sugar daddies or our young boyfriends, we wish the whole sad and sorry bunch of you much joy with each other.

There's a funny ending to my relationship with Toby Young. After he'd closed down the *Modern Review* – which as I write is about to rise like a particularly brilliant phoenix from the ashes of his career – we no longer spoke except through the newspapers, which called us ceaselessly for comments on the situation. I'm afraid that at one point, rather high on myself, I said a very silly, conceited and vainglorious thing, I think to *The Times*: 'As for Toby Young, he's finished here now. And he'd better get out of town quick, if he knows what's good for him, like everyone else who's ever crossed me.'

They hadn't, of course.

But he did!

Half-way up the Nineties – until 26 January 1995, to be precise –

I was well and truly laid low, with Grouchoitis, so low that I couldn't even limbo under my own thin line of self-respect. That is, I was surrounded by people with no soul, no politics and no purpose in life beyond ascertaining where the next line of coke was coming from. And I was slowly but surely becoming one of them – the biggest one of all, in fact, as I always had to be. Hell, listen, for all I know it's entirely possible that I could have *made* them like that, that it was *my* malign and shimmering influence which transformed that merry band of boys and girls from brave, crusading young bloods, who spent their days at work on the Great Humanitarian Novel and their nights bouncing between the Rape Crisis Centre, the Samaritans and the Donkey Sanctuary, to slavering cokehounds who knew nothing much was certain beyond the fact that they'd wake up with sticky white stuff in every orifice the following morning. But – heh heh heh – I DON'T THINK SO.

If I must compare myself to a child's toy at this point, I'd say I was a Slinkee; not a Barbie Doll or an Action Man nor even a Magic Slate, but a Slinkee. Becoming a Slinkee was a more or less unavoidable side-effect of Grouchoitis; because of the late nights and hungover mornings and hair of the Bolivian dog that bit you, you'd be all wound up pretty much all the time. But you wouldn't be wound up to any useful ends, like writing Hangover Square or arriving at the Finland Station with nothing but a headful of dreams and the clothes you stood up in – oh no! You'd be all wound up in a totally *aimless* sort of way just like a silly old Slinkee stumbling down an endless flight of stairs.

Every morning I woke early, feeling sick; every morning back then seemed to be a morning after, a morning sickness, a sickness of mourning for my one and only, only-looking life. I would sleepwalk into the kitchen, collect my cleaning materials and do housework for hours, polishing my black ash work table until I could see my sad, sorry, could-do-better face in it. And that was it; my work. My work table polished to perfection, I would go back to bed.

I became scared to touch my typewriter, for fear of what fresh swill would flow from my fingertips. My brain appeared to have a tapeworm lodging in it. Since the age of nineteen, when Peter York (after my dear deified Dad, definitely the most important man in my life *ever*) first spotted me across a crowded *NME*, I had become used to being referred to as one of the cleverest women in Britain. In my teens and twenties I had a photographic memory and a brain like a mischievous computer; I could feed in ribbons of information about, say, the Futurists, the Viet Cong and the Grunwick strike and pull out of my hat some fantastic tapestry, shimmering with profundity.

Now, whatever I fed in, I pulled out the most trivial tripe imaginable; the new names that British sitcoms were given when adapted for the American small screen, for instance, or a complete list of Jayne Mansfield's husbands. Towards the end, I couldn't even get *that* right; I started getting Mickey Hargitay and Matt Cimber the wrong way round. The cleverest woman in Britain (which to me had always meant *the world*) was only slightly more sentient than a punnet of Wimbledon strawberries. And – hey! – I had *done it all myself*! Give that girl a medal!

I truly felt like King Midas in reverse; everything I touched turned to drink, to dust, to ashes. But every night I would paint on a smile and get it up again; when it came to faking an erection, no one could fill a condom the way I could, and every night with the aid of various substances I came to a riotous climax across the Hot Table at the Groucho Club where the prettiest, bitterest boys and girls in London lounged beside me, flanking me like Ma Barker's babes, except these kids carried Filofaxes rather than carbines. I thought they were protecting me. Looking back, it seems more likely that they were guarding me; guarding me, that is, as in keeping me for themselves. They didn't want anyone else to have me. Especially if that anyone else was me.

But then I met Charlotte, who saved my life.

'You thought you were in a bar, surrounded by your friends. But you were in a cage and your friends were *the bars.'*

It was just another Groucho party and all around me the usual suspects desperately sought something, anything, to make the blood, or at least the Pacemaker, race. I had set up my cage cosily in the corner and was being guarded by Will Self, Tom Shone and Toby Young. I had become quite friendly with my guards, and we chatted quite amicably about this and that, the state of the nation and the shocking price of drugs, until Will Self spotted Nick Hornby across the room.

'It's that fucking wanker with the football!'

'Will, Will . . .' soothed Tom, a friend of both of them. A right little ray of sunshine, in fact. A friend to all the world and his wife. Especially his wife. 'Calm down . . .'

'Calm down, man? He dissed The Novel!' It was true; Nick had written something about how no one with any talent wanted to write literary novels any more, using me and his bro-in-law Robert Harris as examples, published in the *Sunday Times* the previous week. (This was before *High Fidelity* claimed squatter's rights in the best-seller charts, heh heh.) 'No one disses The Novel! The Novel is . . . hey, wait for me, man!' Will croaked, suddenly espying one of his drug buddies about to visit the powder room alone.

'We weren't introduced. We recognised each other.'

So I was sitting there minding my own business when all at once, out of nowhere, into the big blue of my amazing shrinking life, a girl from an Erté illustration plunged deep into the slip-stream of my subconscious and surfaced smiling, sleek with significance.

At last. It was Charlotte R.

'What kept you?'

Charlotte R, it transpired, was the twenty-five-year-old daughter of a millionaire (is there any sweeter job description, you may wonder, of one's love object?) who had once alarmed her mother, grandmother and then-boyfriend by entering their blameless Sussex sitting-room at a canter one sunshiny day waving a book of my essays like a young Red Guard with a Mao cookbook yelling something along the lines of 'I'll have her, I will!' And had I well and truly was.

Most kisses send you to sleep; all the better to keep you. But in the space of Charlotte's first kiss, I recalled my dreams and

dreamed my future, and then I woke up. My first words were: 'Oh
. . . I *remember* . . .' I won't forget again.

What a relief it is, finally to be *known*. It took Charlotte R less
than a year to know me more thoroughly than I have ever been
known in my life, all the way in. When she touched me it was as if
she was reading Braille, and under her hands I became an open
book, a book that turned its own pages and illuminated itself
when it grew dark, and even scribbled notes in its own margins:
good evil bit coming up here, Charlotte! She looked upon it all and
never once flinched – though she later told me that she felt distinctly sick a couple of times. Still, you can't make a heroine without breaking legs.

I'm not a modest type, especially, but I couldn't believe how interested people were when I eloped with Charlotte. Not that we're
not the most fascinating and scintillating people I know – we are.
But still. You'd think people in the media would have the artifice
by now not to display their own dreariness and lack of lives by the
rabid interest they showed in ours. Never mind – bless 'em.

We emerged on May Day 1995 from the sumptuous Gothic
gloom of the Library Suite at Blake's Hotel, blissed out and blink-
ing, to repair to her love nest in West Kensington, little knowing
what lay ahead. Charlotte shared a flat with Jessica Aitkenhead,
now a *Guardian* columnist, who was then a trainee journalist of
only twenty-five and robustly heterosexual. She wasn't especially
sensitive and cheerfully claimed – boasted, even – never to have
been in love, yet she said the loveliest thing to me when I first met
her, when Charlotte and I were still simply dating.

She recalled Charlotte arriving back at the flat after only our
second meeting, one afternoon when we had gone to see the film I
had to review for the *Sunday Times* that week. It was, with supersonic suitability, *Heavenly Creatures*, the story of two superbright
misfit girls who fall in love and commit murder, and was to stand
as the celluloid model for our love with Toby Young's reputation
standing in for the unfortunate victim. After that we'd gone to the
Groucho and drunk Sea Breezes and, without warning, Charlotte

took my right hand, stuck my first two fingers in her mouth and started sucking them, staring me in the eye all the time. Then her eyelids fluttered and closed, her small red mouth still sucking.

I couldn't *believe* it! In broad daylight! I started to giggle, amazed.

I could get to *like* this, no problem!

Anyway, after an hour or so we went our separate ways – so far as we were able. I walked into my Bloomsbury rooms and smiled at my husband.

'Are you on Ecstasy?' he enquired.

'Yessss,' I breathed, wandering off.

Meanwhile, across town, Charlotte had walked into her flat to find Jessica – Decca – watching MTV. She sat there smiling, Jessica said, as though in a trance. When the Rolling Stones – of all people – started singing 'Angie', Charlotte burst into tears. 'Oh, Dec, her *hands*! She had *ink* on her *hands*!'

'And I watched her crying,' said Jessica, 'and I knew, Julie, that that was the way I wanted to feel about someone more than anything on earth. But I knew I never would.'

Jessica's brashness and lack of sensitivity was really just what was needed in a girl who suddenly found herself sharing a flat with what appeared to all intents and purposes to be two lesbians in love. Often she would return home late from the *Independent* and burst blondely into the front room to find me in a black lace slip on the sofa, 'Slide Away' on the stereo and Charlotte in nothing but a black bra on top of me, giving it some serious wrist action. Dec would simply kick off her cowboy boots, talking a mile a minute, flop down on the sofa, watch *Coronation Street*, then dash off to a night-club to dance for eight hours straight. Charlotte and I would remain frozen *en tableaux*, maintaining eye contact, only to resume play when the door slammed. It was the sexiest sitcom not to make it past the censors come to life.

We were living our dream, spending our evenings making love and scrapbooks. We were happy as idiots and sexy as rabbits. But we were living slap bang in the middle of Mediaville, and I was Queen of the Groucho; 'You're the Queen and I'm the Princess;

the Princess serves the Queen,' Charlotte pointed out reasonably one evening when I felt she was being over-solicitous of my comfort. Something had to give – rather, to be given away.

Charlotte was a fussy eater but a frequent one, and of a morning I loved nothing more than to slide out of bed while she slept, slip into my slacks and sun-glasses and raincoat, and stroll down to the Londis on the corner to purchase a fine if eclectic early-morning repast for her: gummy cola bottle sweets washed down with Coca Cola was a big favourite, I recall, though she could also be tempted by seaweed and bean curd, and she would eat beetroots like other people eat apples.

It was a sunny day in May and despite the recent upheavals in my life I felt truly 'centred', as the Americans say. It is one of the profound pleasures of life, I feel, to leave one's lover sleeping and go shopping for food. It's to do with being a hunter-gatherer. Or greedy. Or something. I sang one of Our Songs softly as I strolled along. Charlotte and I being mega-girls, and this being a mega-love, we had not one Our Song but close on thirty, including 'A Girl Like You'. 'I've never met a girl like you before . . . this old town's changed so much . . . don't feel like I belong . . . too many protest singers . . . not enough protest songs . . . and now *you* come along . . . yeah, now *you* come along . . . and I've never met a girl like you before!'

I turned a leafy Kensington Corner and heard a cry of 'Julie!'

I twisted round. A man with a camera was running towards me. I'd never been doorstepped before, but it was sheer instinct, instinct learned from a million paparazzi pictures (the Janet and John – Jackie and Joan! – books of the glamour-hungry, dispossessed young person) which made me hold my handbag up in front of my face and run back past him the way I had come.

He ran after me. 'Julie! I need a picture!'

'Get lost!' I yelled, still teetering along in my stilettos, handbag against face.

'But I'm from the *paper*!' His voice was amazingly depressed and wheedling. 'I'm from the *paper*!'

Why this should have made me stop in my tracks, shoulder my

bag, stick out my chest and say 'Cheese!' I'll never know. I later learned he was from the *Daily Mail*, which made sense: *the* paper of sex-starved curtain-twitchers, madly beating their collective meat over the sexual adventures of those prettier and braver than they, while pretending to disapprove violently. But I had never even worked for them; why his desperate cry 'But I'm from the *paper*'? I think that there might just have been a chance that he could see how scummy and unworthy of a higher species his behaviour was and was doing all he could to signal that it hadn't been his idea.

I gained access to Charlotte's lobby and raced up the stairs to her flat. Once there, I ran into the bedroom and jumped on to the bed. She woke up, rubbed her eyes and held out her arms straight away, smiling. 'It's my *baby*!'

'Guess what? I've just been *doorstepped*!'

'You're *joking*!' We rushed to her bedroom window and crawled on to the balcony. Through the bars we could see Sad Camera Man squinting up at the building, no doubt imagining us up to all sorts of Sapphic salaciousness and wishing he could take a few snap-shots. '*Amazing*!'

We sat back to consider. 'Well, we can't stay in here for ever,' I pointed out.

'Bloody right! There's the dry cleaning for one thing.' Dry cleaning looms large in same-sex romances; I think they're far cleaner than stinky heteros.

'And it's *such* a beautiful day.' It was, too; a real scorcher by now.

'Right!' Charlotte scampered to her feet and over to her closet. She began throwing clothes on to the floor. 'Ah! Gotcha!'

Dressed in the tightest black jeans I had ever seen and a skintight Dolce Gabbana bra top, black sun-glasses and Ginza Red lipstick, groomed to within an inch of her life, Charlotte nipped out 'casually' to the dry cleaners round the corner. When she got back I was made up and sewn into a dark-blue short summer dress.

'Right, you'll do.' She nodded. 'Let's go out to lunch.'

'Did he follow you?'

'He was asleep in his car, the cretin.' She laughed. 'He's not

now, though. I tapped on the window on my way back. Come on.'
She kissed me. 'We're coming out.'

Sure enough Sad Camera Man was there at the ready and pretty
quick on the draw this time. She took me by the wrist, I raised my
other hand to shield my eyes, Charlotte stared straight into the lens
and *snap*! – that photograph of the bold, beautiful girl leading the
leading lady into the light was brought to life. You can call it
doorstepping, invasion of privacy, whatever you like – but if you
look closely, you can see me smiling.

Charlotte and I between us had the four best legs in London. In
fact, the only thing that had better legs than us was the story,
which proceeded to run and run. Lust in the bedroom met,
mugged and merged with loathing in the boardroom as the *Modern
Review*, the little magazine with big ideas which Toby Young and
I had founded two years previously and which had during that
time eaten up most of my disposable income, was 'torched' by Mr
Young rather than handing over the reins to Charlotte and me.

The idea had been to produce a magazine which would look like
F. R. Leavis was editing *Smash Hits* at its peak. Two years later
Toby was no longer a bright-eyed boy attractive to glamour girls
like Natascha McElhone and Sam de Teran, but a balding man
who paid Shepherd's Bush prostitutes, and naturally his steward-
ship was affected by his growing rancidity; he went from Leavis to
Beavis, with his wizened henchman Edward Porter as his trusty
Butthead. By the time Charlotte and I pointed out that we were
way off course, we were selling a teeny fraction of what we had at
our high-handed best and, worse than that, all semblance of wit
and wisdom was gone. Instead, thanks to Toby, it might better
have been renamed Model Review, incorporating Wank Weekly
and Tit Quarterly.

So, rather than let us have it, Toby torched it. This was incredibly low, considering the money we had been lucky enough to get
many media and advertising figures to invest in us. The papers
went wild. The combination of cunnilingus and corruption, fucking and feuding, kissing and dissing, was far too much to expect
the self-obsessed circle-jerkers of the print media to put up even a

token resistance to. They made total pigs of themselves – with our love as the trough. We were headlines, we were cartoons – we were even the subject of a front-line account by Decca, who wrote a charming piece for the *Independent*. 'First to arrive were letters, great packets of them thumping on to the mat every morning. Then came lilies, armfuls and armfuls of lilies. Finally came six crates of Coca Cola – it was clearly the real thing. Then came a word processor, a bust of Lenin and a mystery brunette. Julie Burchill had come to stay.'

'Ah!' said the nice Indian man at Londis the week after the piece appeared. 'You are one of the famous Three Girls In A Flat!' Indeed I was.

Some people's reaction to my situation amazed me with its denseness. I was a columnist for the *Sunday Times*, and the week after the story broke one of the corporate bully boys rang me up and demanded to know why I hadn't given my own paper an exclusive.

'What? On me and Charlotte?'

'Of course!'

'But Anthony, I was *doorstepped*. I was *outed*. Surely you didn't expect me to doorstep myself?'

'You have a responsibility to your newspaper. A responsibility which you have failed to honour.' With that killer blow, he hung up. I was obviously supposed to do the decent thing, go into the library and shoot myself.

I gaped at the phone. Pompous old git! I wondered if he'd told Andrew Neil that *he'd* had a responsibility to doorstep himself when the Pamella Bordes story broke – that was a big one and no mistake. But I bet he hadn't.

If you're two women in love, everybody wants to have a look – a little poke and a prod, metaphorically if not literally (though most of them wouldn't have said no to that, either). The fantasy of two girls making love to each other as an opening act for the main attraction (heh heh) of some ugly old cock is so entrenched in the male psyche that when they find out that a couple of girls are going at it like knives through I-Can't-Believe-It's-Not-Butter, they

179

really do think it's a come-on. Well, in our case it wasn't. In our case it was a go–away.

Then the men you know go through this endless business of claiming that you're not *really* lesbians. Fair enough; we never really thought we were. I was a Charlottist and Charlotte was a Juliette.

'Does this mean you're off men, because you're with Charlotte?' said Beverly D'Silva of *Cosmopolitan* when she called to ask me to write something about young male sex symbols.

I thought about it. 'Well, basically, Beverly, I suppose it means I'm off everyone but Charlotte.'

This seemed to me a pretty obvious definition of being in love; you don't fancy *anyone* else. If a heterosexual girl were in love with a man, I'd expect *her* to 'go off' men as well, apart from the one she was in love with.

'Miss Raven and I are not lesbians; we are simply in love,' I wrote to the *Evening Standard* when they reported that we had had a Coming Out Party, which had in fact been a welcome back party for our Manchester friend Asif Noorani, who had recently had a frank and free exchange of views with a strange car in the early hours of the morning. Richard Young, the paparazzi pasha, waited for hours in the street below, buzzing our buzzer repeatedly; Charlotte's brother, Daniel, was doorstepped by reporters on his way in.

'What do you think of Julie and Charlotte?'

'I think they're lovely.'

'But you're Charlotte's brother! What do you think of her and Julie being . . . together?'

'I think it's lovely.'

Knowing they were down there, we popped tantalising champagne corks out on the balcony all night long, our beautiful friend Sian Lezard squealing highly audible '*Oooo!*'s each time, like a space cadet turned Sun Stunna. With the party whirling around us, we kissed. Truly, this is what we had wanted all along: to be together, to have fun and to have the eyes of the lousy world on us.

Some idiots who understand nothing have tried to evaluate how important *la publicité* was to us. The *Daily Mail*, in a typically tangibly tumescent full-page piece called OBSESSION!, came to the conclusion that we were only in it for the column inches – a strange conclusion, considering the title. (Maybe they meant we were obsessed with publicity, but I think it's more likely they were just stupid and didn't see the contradiction.)

In truth, it was hard even for Charlotte and me to tell where love ended and ambition began. The glow of our love became the blaze of publicity without missing a (heart)beat. There is a chance that we could have been decent, anonymous, knicker-wearing waitresses, say, or kennel maids, and fallen in love just the same. But I don't know and I don't care. If we hadn't been the sort of girls who were born to be notorious, we wouldn't have been the girls we both fell in love with.

And fall in love we indubitably had, much to the distress of our male friends. Funnily enough, it was those men with the most pornographic imaginations who seemed the most distressed by our good fortune; apparently, when it comes to Hot Dyke Action, when love comes in the door erections fly out the window. Toby, in particular, was utterly inconsolable that his lifetime's fascination and his typist were making sweet music together and actually went to the trouble of drawing me up a *pie chart* to demonstrate to me the tiny fraction my alleged 'bisexuality' played in my physical make-up.

He needn't have bothered. If the idea of calling myself a lesbian seemed naff, the mere notion of being a 'bisexual' made me want to renounce sexual congress for ever and have myself walled up in a nunnery in Nuneaton. Bisexual men are just opportunistic slags and thus simply taking male sexuality to its logical conclusion; they have nothing to answer for and are only doing what comes naturally. Bisexual women, on the other hand, are prick-teasers and prick-pleasers of the worst kind; show me a loud, proud 'bisexual' woman who doesn't end up taking a dick finale nine times out of ten and I'll show you a sarcastic Swede.

Bisexuality proper also indicates some level of confusion and confused is the last thing I have ever been when it comes to sex. I subscribe very much to the Cakeshop Theory of Sexuality: 'I'll have that one!' How much confusion can possibly come into the words 'I Want', which is the one rule I have always lived by when it comes to love? Maybe the cake I've chosen or the cake I've ditched are confused. But hell, they're only cakes!

The people I was married to for the whopping total of sixteen years never really knew me. I was just a cast of corny old characters to them, each one sillier and more clueless than the last. Working-Class Angel, Demon Nympho, Castrating Bitch . . . every one a case of mistaken identity. Perhaps the most preposterous sighting of all could be seen in the (mercifully unpublished) novel by one of them, in which I bring my life to a watery close by jumping off the end of Brighton Pier because I'm too sensitive for this world! Me – too sensitive! Did he have the wrong number, or what? I'm not too sensitive for Hades, let alone this world! Truth to tell, the idea of me thrashing about in the swirling brine made me feel quite insulted. That's not me! I went off him a *lot* right then, I can tell you. (NB I think it was meant to be a *tribute*.)

But Charlotte wasn't interested in making either myth or money out of me, she was interested in saving my life. So she saved it up, day by day, and then she put it in a shiny box tied with a glittering ribbon and handed it back to me and said, that's yours, and it belongs to you, and only to you, and no one will ever take it away from you again.

I just love her. I always will.

Charlotte R was not only beautifully serious – a Marxist, praise the Lord, in a swarming sea of Miscellaneous Men – but seriously beautiful; her body was like a new country, austere yet lawless. One look at her and I knew that she hadn't grown up in what is, for a child, the biggest yet most cramped cage of all – London. Her aspect spoke to me of great, gorgeous horizons and fresh, cool breezes which swept through the cobwebs in my mind and left it clean and serene once more. Of course, she came from Sugartown, my very favourite place in the whole wide world.

'Brighton looks like a town which is helping the police with their enquiries,' Keith Waterhouse once said. 'Brighton is an excellent place in which to restore health – and, once sufficiently braced, in which to ruin it again,' said J. B. Priestley. To me, ever since I was first sent here on newspaper business in 1986, it has looked like a town which has just had a multiple orgasm, while sad grey London looks like a city which has post-coital triste.

Brighton went to my head straight away; sent here to cover the Labour Party Conference in a very junior capacity by the *Mail on Sunday*, I was shown to my room, looked out of the window, couldn't see the sea, turned round and stamped my foot. 'I want a *suite* . . .' I said, and was given one; the Editor's. From the word go, Brighton gave me a licence to be as bad as I wanted to be and as good as I could.

In later years, when I was sickening daily from the strain of being queen of a moribund scene, I would escape at weekends to the Hotel Metropole, where Ralph Gorse gave Esther Downes her first sip of the road to ruin in *The West Pier*. From my suite on the far left of the second floor, I had the absolute optimum view of the ruined pier, from the turning off of the red sign – WEST PIER had by that time become WEST PIE, which detracted somewhat from the tragedy of the situation – to the SAVE ME banner which appeared soon afterwards when all seemed lost. I used to sit out on the balcony all night long, drinking hard, believing that the poor rotting structure was trying to send me a message about myself. SAVE ME: a magnificent ruin. Yeah, you and me both, babe, I would think wearily into my drink. But apparently it looks like we have both been saved, by the skin of our belief.

In Brighton I wake up early too – up at six, even if I went to bed at four – but I do not pace my flat like a big caged cat here, as I did in our nation's glorious capital. Instead, I find myself pulled straight out into the streets, rain or shine, in lipstick, sun-glasses and raincoat, by the very blissed-out, up-for-it power of Brighton itself, into streets washed clean by the smell of the sea. It is the very CLEANLINESS of freedom that strikes me; the freedom to stand on your own feet, meet all your responsibilities and have all your fun. There is no feeling quite like the cleanliness of freedom. The seagulls swirl and cry above me as I walk down West Street to the sea, and they sound so sad that I know they must once have been human and that they were caged Londoners who dreamed of moving here but died before they made it. That's why they cry; they are trapped souls who died in captivity.

I am Brighton's burglar bride; I adore it and I want to steal it. I remember at that first Party Conference I couldn't bring myself to waste a minute of the precious time I had here inside the Brighton Centre, but instead feverishly cased the place all day long, up and down the sea-front, wondering if there was *any* way I could possibly take it home with me. But now it *is* home and, every morning when I walk down the hill towards that big blue, I feel so happy I could cry. Sometimes, if I couldn't get out and see it that day, at first I'd panic. But now I realise that its beauty isn't finite, like every other beauty I've known, and that it will still go on without me. It sounds mad and boastful, but I don't think I can say the same of most people I've known. Not *properly*.

This is a BRIGHT town to London's dark. Walking along the esplanade from the waltzing white sweep of Adelaide Crescent, which sometimes appears to be the swirling skirts of Palmeira Square, past the Peace Statue of the sad angel and the War Memorial which honours sad angels, past the big hotels where I first came to feel that I could come home to a place where I had never lived, to the big, brassy Palace Pier where the machines play the people, I feel sheer, shimmering love for this town. Walking along the sea-front, you can see how Brighton visibly and literally *opens up*, as you always hope your life will, probably until your dying day. Walking along Oxford Street, or Bond Street, or the King's Road, you can feel London closing in on you, as you fear your life will, and you're probably right. My life has closed twice already; I don't intend to let it happen again until the Man Upstairs rings the red velvet curtain down.

The sweetest words in the world; it's got to be a toss-up between the announcement, every eight minutes past the hour at Victoria Station, 'The train now standing at Platform 16 is the Capital-Coast Express, stopping at East Croydon and then fast to Brighton

only. *Brighton only*.' That and, 'But Julie, you *are* the Spirit of
Brighton!' as spoken by the Mayor of Brighton, Mr Ian Duncan.
But no, Ian, not its Spirit; its Burglar Bride. I came to steal, and fell
in love – with a whole town. Le Corbusier said that a house should
be a machine for living. Brighton is a machine for living, loving and
leaving your sorrow behind. London, on the other hand, is a
machine for dying. Slowly.

Despite all the swinging London Mark 2 hype, I just feel *so sorry*
for all the ex-*compadres* who scold me for leaving. But who would-
n't hitch a ride off the *Titanic* if they got the chance? The fact they
can't stomach is that I came to Brighton not to *escape* the Fast Life,
as is usual in deserters to the Home Counties, but to find a *faster*
one – one not based around sitting in gridlocks and rotting in the
Groucho. And I've found it. I'll tell you one thing: if London *does*
swing, then it swings only in the manner of a hanged man.
Swinging, swinging, *swung*.

In the meantime, ain't *we* got fun.

Having found a place that I could finally call home – because home
is not where you came from, but where you choose to go – it was
time to go back and hear the Bristol Sound one more time. In the
final massive irony, the Bristol Sound – so long coming! – was the
sound-track to my best and brightest love, as my Brighton girl and
I swooned the springtime nights away to Massive Attack, Tricky
and Portishead. 'You're the book that I have opened . . . and now
I've got to know much more' . . . 'You're sure you want to be with
me? I've nothing to give. No law will say this love is blessed' . . .
'Nobody *loves* me, it's true; not like you do . . .'

'Do you feel sophisticated?' my editor, Charlotte M, asked me the
other day. My answer was immediate and completely instinctive,
surprising even myself with its unforced affirmation.

I threw back my head and laughed. '*I'll* say!'

It was smart and sensitive of her to ask this question, because of
course *being sophisticated* was the Holy Grail of my youth. Every
Sobranie smoked, every dog orgy lied about in my Secret Sex

Diary, every Biba lipstick applied that made me look as though I had recently suffered frostbite – sophistication was both the spur and the glittering prize. My parents were political and they were clever; it was sophistication, which they saw no use for and I thought a sublime achievement, which had separated us at birth. (Mine.)

Well, I well and truly feel sophisticated now. I'm certainly not the provincial child who believed that you could get cancer from pressing your navel too hard. I can change a fuse, deflower virgins so exquisitely that they're mine for life and tell the perfect lie. Yes, I guess I am. I have been sexually shocked only once in the past seven years: when my friend Angie The Dominatrix came back from a club toilet fussing about her complicated leather costume. 'Girl, it took me half an hour to get out of this thing. And there wasn't even a man there to *drink* it!'

But the real acid test of my sophistication is that I know this system was born to die. *Die, do you hear?* Forget all your black dresses and cigarette holders, surely only a hoosier of the corniest order can believe that Communism will never walk the earth again. Well, we *will*. Quite soon – and this time, we're coming to *your* house *first*.

Why did I ever think my parents were the enemy? A year after thoroughly shaming them in both tabloid and broadsheet press by leaving my perfect marriage in order to run off with a *girl – the* girl – they welcomed me with open arms, hearts and minds. Why did I ever think they would do anything else? And how, having finally comprehended how wonderful they are, am I ever expected to live without them when they die?

Because, more than any scrappy little thing I may have accomplished by myself, my main achievement is that I was the child of *that* marriage, *that* happiness, *that* nobility. Many parents are bad, and some – mostly men – are *evil*; that in our time this can at last be acknowledged outside of a book of Grimms' fairy-tales, and even pursued and prosecuted unto the COD of suicide on the part of the evil-doer, is a great and terrible beauty. But sometimes it seems that every living family is dysfunctional. Mothers are cold. Fathers are distant. Granny wore a beard and Granpa wore Balenciaga. You saw Mommy kissing Santa Claus and Daddy having unsafe sex with Donner and Blitzen. The depoliticizing of our society has seen its completion in the triumph of the personal relationship as the one deciding factor of our fate. But not for me.

They were lucky to get me – but then, I was lucky to get them. More than anything else, I wanted this book, the story of my life, to express the strange glory of my parents; parents without whom I honestly believe it would be impossible for me to carry on. From the time I became obsessed with being *myself*, all I wanted was to escape them. Now, irretrievably myself, they are my end, my whole ambition.

Some people, Americans, say you can never go home again. Myself, I think it's more likely that you can never really leave.

Born Slippy

'It is a sign of real genius that it remains unspoilt by success,' says Martin Esslin and, twenty-one years after I first put pen to paper for pleasure and profit, I *still* write like an angel on Angel Dust. Which is not to say it's always easy. Getting one's talent going can be quite troublesome; I always see *my* struggle in terms of those Fifties films where a hunk in a letter-sweater is trying to get Sandra Dee to come across:

ME (*to Talent*) Oh, come on, honey!

TALENT (*firmly*) No.

ME Oh, come on, honey. You *know* you'll like it once we get going.

TALENT No, I can't. You'll hate me afterwards.

ME Oh, come on, baby! Did I hate you after *No Exit* sold only six copies? When our *Screen One* refused at the final fence? When we were so rudely ejected from the *Sunday Express* for making Middle England choke on its All Bran by suggesting that a child is statistically safer from sexual abuses left alone overnight with a strange lesbian than with its own blood father and other such outlandish propositions? Did I?

TALENT (*weakening*) Well . . . no . . .

ME See? Look, just let me put the paper in for a minute . . . just

the teeny weeny *tip* of it into the machine – I promise I'll take it
out if you don't like it.

TALENT   Well . . .

ME (*sensing victory*)   Come on – tell you what, how about a
drink?

TALENT   I really shouldn't . . .

ME   Just an incy wincy dry Martini, babe – and then see how
you feel . . .

Now, nine times out of ten, talent will just turn over and go to
sleep. But once in a while, *once in a while*, talent will get that meat
in its mouth and suck the juice right out of the thing; go baby go!

The secret of my success is that I always wanted to be a writer,
and it showed; unlike the other contenders, I didn't join the pop
press because I wanted to be a pop star or sleep with pop stars or
buy drinks for pop stars or be a TV presenter or travel or any of the
other dumb beauty queen reasons ninety-five per cent of people
join the pop press. I wanted to write, and writing for the *New
Musical Express* was simply the first offer of paid employment that
came my way. Love has no pride.

People seem to think that words are these easily led bimbos you
can use just to get you where you want to go – but it's never been
so. Words are as smart as you and me – well, smart as me and
smarter than you, most likely – and if your ambition lies beyond
them, if you mutter the wrong name at the crucial moment – 'TV!'
– they just won't give you the best of their love. They'll become
hookers and they won't kiss you. And if words won't kiss you,
you're fucked. So to speak.

So later, much later, when the banging has stopped and the
courier has come and gone, Talent and I lie panting on the bed, and
I turn to it as I light a black Sobranie.

ME   How was it for you, darling?

TALENT (*snapping*)   Lousy – I'm sick to death of your cheap
stylistic devices. They were bad enough when you were nineteen, but now? You must be the oldest juvenile lead in the

racket! And anyway, *why* do you bother – you *know* those subs couldn't derive full job satisfaction anywhere outside of an abattoir in the rush hour. Don't come crying to *me* when you're suffering death by a thousand cuts, that's all!

Once you've been married for a certain amount of time, you start to notice things about people that irritate you. The sound of mastication must be one of the nastiest ever known to human ears, and obviously the reason why the television and, after a decent period of time, the TV dinner were invented. The common married practice of eating dinner while watching one's favourite television soap has kept more marriages intact than the entire stock of any given Ann Summers shop ever could. And when we *do* observe the human animal eating without benefit of televisual camouflage, we can see that he makes a very nasty noise indeed. This is called the Dinner Party and it is when we observe our mates at such gatherings – loud, boorish, boring – that we often really do start to think that it's time we made like a red T-shirt chucked in the washer with some white undies. And *ran.*

So far as I can make out from the behaviour of my cohabitees over the years – Tony, Cosmo and Charlotte, bless 'em! – my nastiest habit (apart from running off and leaving them) is laughing at my own writing, as I'm writing it. You'd think people would be happy for the people they *say* they love to find such repleteness, such satisfaction, such hilarity right there in their own backyard, wouldn't you? If laughter *is* a good thing, as we've always been brought up to believe, why not get yours direct and cut out the middle man? But to judge from the mean little faces and sudden attacks of the Butterfingers (thus occasioning molto slamming doors) abounding at such an occurrence, this is not and never was the case.

If they *do* love me, why aren't people happy seeing me the happiest I can get? – i.e. giving myself a right proper funny-bone bashing. OK, I'll admit that on a few occasions in the past (when I was still funny, heh heh) my laughter would sometimes be loud and immodest, robust enough perhaps to wake my beloveds from deep slumber at 2.30 a.m. But this was the exception that proved the rule. It is true that on one, and only one, occasion – while writing my television *Screen One* film *Prince*, coincidentally – I felt beholden to lie down on the floor and howl like a dog at what I had written. But I must stress again that it was *just the once*.

I suppose I *can* see why people object to this lovable little glitch I've got, though I really do believe it says more about them than it does about me. It may well be that such sublime self-amusement is slightly parasexual and rather rude, in both senses of the word. I do not know. But I would ask them to correct the mote in their own eye before they cast aspersions at the tear of laughter in mine. And to put aside their feelings of jealousy and rejection for just one minute in order to ask themselves this question. If I'm all I need to get by – as it would appear I am – at least I'm never going to turn round one day like loads of women do and say 'You never talk to me any more. We never laugh any more!' Because I'll have been talking and laughing away like anything. And I'll probably never notice that they weren't.

'Success and failure are both difficult to endure,' said Joseph Heller in 1975. 'Along with success come drugs, divorce, fornication, bullying, meditation, medication, depression, neurosis and suicide. With failure comes failure.' I love that; it's the perfect antidote to all those self-loathing pronouncements from types like Truman Capote and Oscar Wilde and Saint Teresa of Avila – who would *not* have been fun on a houseparty – such as 'more tears are shed over answered prayers than unanswered ones' and 'the only thing worse than not getting your heart's desire is getting it'. *Sisters, this is a lie put about to keep you down*; getting what you want is nothing less than wonderful and don't let *anyone* tell you otherwise.

My twenty-one years in the hack racket have found me compared with many people from Dorothy Parker to Goebbels, via Jane Russell and Gillian Anderson, while once in the same week in the Eighties I was described as a 'Marxist critic' by *Encounter* and a 'Right-wing columnist' by the *Independent*. Either of which will suit me fine; as James Dean said when asked if he was bisexual, 'Well, I'm not going to go through life with one hand behind my back.' That's the way I feel about politics.

It's nice being called the cleverest woman in Britain (*Observer*) or more influential than Vanessa Redgrave, Kim Wilde and the Princess of Wales rolled into one (Ray Gosling, Radio 4 – well, it *was* the Eighties) but the *real* kick – and this sounds really mindless teenybopper stuff, but it can't be helped – is knowing that YOUR HEROES HAVE HEARD OF YOU.

When Phillip Knightley went on one of his periodic visits to Kim Philby in Moscow, this time to persuade him to co-operate on a new book, he found the greatest living Englishman in maudlin mood. 'You don't want to write a book about me, old man. The young people don't know who I am any more.' In a bid to convince him otherwise, Mr Knightley gave him a collection of recent writings on himself, one of them by me.

Months later, when Mr Knightley returned, the G.L.E. pulled the piece from his wallet and waved it at his putative interviewer. 'OK, old man – you've convinced me.' That I was known, even by proxy, to my last hero, makes me happier than any number of digits, no matter how extravagantly arranged; it takes me right back to all the teenage nights when I cried myself to sleep because Marc Bolan didn't know my name. I got what I wanted.

Journalism is still a hideously middle-class profession and I'm proud that I made it from where I did. It amuses me to see old Fleet Street hands as diverse as Keith Waterhouse and Professor Norman Stone take my ideas on board and enlarge on them, just the way the young bloods on the pop and style press did with my interest in everything from the Soviet Union to Burt Bacharach before them. I still get letters from teenagers asking *how I did it*, and I still enjoy telling them that I did it by *not* going to journalism school, *not* getting an education and *not* training in the provinces as the NUJ always demanded and still advises. Feet first into the legend, that's the only way to go.

How did I do it? One school of thought says luck, but what people often mean by luck is that you made it look effortless, like an ice-skater gliding up to a 10:10:10 finish, and you can only make it look effortless if you have a *lot* of talent. Probably my greatest gift, apart from my talent itself ('Ha! Credit at last!' – Talent) and my big green eyes, has been this: an ability to combine the *modus operandi* of the simpleton with the perceptions of the intellectual – essential, I think you'll agree, if one isn't going to stay stuck dithering in the morbid margins of the modern world for ever.

I want a quiet life and a big-noise career, so I shall continue to wander through the global village like the global village idiot savant I am, keeping an eye peeled for the next main chance to combine pleasure and profit. Having slept with a Jew, taken drugs and been famous, I now maintain that I have no ambition.

But then, the last person to say that was Napoleon.

There you go, then. You can wash your hands now. I hope I didn't make you feel *too* dirty. But if I did, it's nothing that won't come out in the wash.

Professor Roger Scruton once wrote of me: 'Often she reads as though she is taking off her knickers and throwing them in your face. Yet it's the reader who feels undressed.' I hope it didn't come to such an undignified tussle between you and me this time round but, hey, that's the breaks.

So I'm off now, off to write in my Book Of Evil Thoughts. But I've loved doing this. And thank you for listening. Who knows, I may even do it again.

And next time, I may even tell the truth.